GW00976404

MARCH

The
Birthstone Petite
Collection

By Suzanne Siegel Zenkel

Design and illustration by
Mullen and Katz

PETER PAUPER PRESS, INC.
WHITE PLAINS · NEW YORK

Special thanks to
Lois L. Kaufman and
Claudine Gandolfi for their
editorial assistance

Contents

A Month Like No Other

March Celebrities
and What They
Have to Say

Parties, Cakes,
Candles, Flowers, and
Birthstones

March
A Month Like No Other

YOUR BIRTHSTONE IS THE
Aquamarine

AND YOUR SPECIAL FLOWER IS THE
Daffodil

It is the first mild day of March:
Each minute sweeter than before,
The redbreast sings from the tall larch
That stands beside our door.

There is a blessing in the air,
Which seems a sense of joy to yield
To the bare trees,
and mountains bare;
And grass in the green field.

WILLIAM WORDSWORTH

How sublime to be born in the month that comes in like a lion and goes out like a lamb! How promising to be brought into the world in the same month that brings in the Springtime—when sunshine abounds and awakens within us a renewed sense of joy. Robert Browning captured the feel of March when he wrote: *The year's at the spring / And day's at the morn . . . / God's in His Heaven— / All's right with the world.*

Why do people, animals, and plants come to life again in March? Why do green buds swell and sap begin to flow in the trees? Why do songbirds appear?

In the Northern Hemisphere, Spring starts with the *vernal equinox*, which occurs on March 20th or 21st. The sun rises directly in the east and sets directly in the west, making day and night exactly the same length in all parts of the Earth. In the northern half of the world, Spring beckons us to enjoy sunshine and the out-of-doors.

If you have a $5.00 bill in your pocket or purse, Abraham Lincoln will be looking back at you now. That was not true on March 10, 1862, the day the United States printed its first paper money, when Alexander Hamilton's likeness appeared on the $5.00 bill.

While no U.S. national holidays fall in March, everybody wants to be Irish on the 17th, St. Patrick's

Day, honoring the patron saint of Ireland, who introduced Christianity into the Emerald Isle. The entire month of March is recognized as National Women's History Month, and includes Universal Women's Week. Both International (Working) Women's Day and United Nations International Women's Day are celebrated on March 8th.

March might well become known in the future as "Jurisprudence Month." Its 31 days encompass the birthdays of five U.S. Supreme Court Justices: Oliver Wendell Holmes (March 8),

Antonin Scalia (March 11), Ruth Bader Ginsburg (March 15), Earl Warren (March 19), and Sandra Day O'Connor (March 26).

The perfect way to relax on a March 10th (and the rest of the month) might be to make a few phone calls in honor of the first telephone message transmitted by Alexander Graham Bell on that day in 1876. Enjoy a plate of pasta sprinkled with the nut of the month, in celebration of National Noodle Month and National Peanut Month.

And just a page away, March babies, are the birth dates and selected wit and wisdom of a host of this month's other birthday celebrants.

March Celebrities and What They Have to Say

March 1

GLENN MILLER, 1904

DINAH SHORE, 1917

HARRY BELAFONTE, 1927

March 1

I like my [gray] hair. I want to be
the meanest senior on the block. I
want people to look at me and say,
"That old guy could be a problem!"

ROBERT CONRAD, 1935

ALAN THICKE, 1947
RON HOWARD, 1954

March 2

SAM HOUSTON, 1793
MELISSA BURTON CORAY, 1828

You're only old once!

DR. SEUSS
(THEODOR GEISEL), 1904

March 2

DESI ARNAZ, 1917

JENNIFER JONES, 1919

JOHN IRVING, 1942

JOHN BON JOVI, 1962

March 3

Mr. Watson, come here, I want you.

ALEXANDER GRAHAM BELL, 1847
First telephone transmission

JEAN HARLOW, 1911

LEE RADZIWILL, 1933

JACKIE JOYNER-KERSEE, 1962

March 6

MICHELANGELO, 1475

I hear the birthday's noisy bliss
My sister's woodland glee,
My father's praise I did not miss
When stooping down,
he cared to kiss
The poet on his knee. . . .

ELIZABETH BARRETT
BROWNING, 1806

March 6

Lou Costello, 1906

Ed McMahon, 1923

Gabriel Garcia-Marquez, 1928

Thomas Foley, 1929

Rob Reiner, 1945

March 6

I'm just a big kid right now,
and I'm in no hurry to grow up.

SHAQUILLE O'NEAL, 1972

March 7

Lord Snowdon,
Anthony Armstrong-Jones, 1930

Willard Scott, 1934

Janet Guthrie, 1938

Michael Eisner, 1942

Ivan Lendl, 1960

March 8

A word is the skin
of a living thought.

OLIVER WENDELL HOLMES, 1841

CYD CHARISSE, 1923
CHARLEY PRIDE, 1938
LYNN REDGRAVE, 1943
AIDAN QUINN, 1959

March 9

AMERIGO VESPUCCI, 1451
JOYCE VAN PATTEN, 1934

Failure is part of success.
Don't be afraid to make a fool
of yourself—I am often
outrageous at readings.
Take risks.
It opens you to greatness.

RAUL JULIA, 1940

March 9

Trish Van Devere, 1943

Charles Gibson, 1943

Bobby Fischer, 1943

March 10

A combination of discipline and
learning leads to confidence.
Remember that everyone is a begin-
ner at some point in his life; even
your teacher was once a pupil.

CHUCK NORRIS, 1940

❧

JASMINE GUY, 1964
PRINCE EDWARD, 1964

March 11

LAWRENCE WELK, 1903

You have to be what you are. If you're constantly trying to project some model—whether it's a model of decorum or of intelligence—people can see right through you.

SAM DONALDSON, 1934

ANTONIN SCALIA, 1936
BOBBY MCFERRIN, 1950

March 12

WALTER M. SCHIRRA, JR., 1923
EDWARD ALBEE, 1928
ANDREW YOUNG, 1932
AL JARREAU, 1940

I believe in grabbing at
happiness . . . if you have to pay
later for a decision you've made,
that's all right.

LIZA MINNELLI, 1946

JAMES TAYLOR, 1948

March 13

WALTER ANNENBERG, 1908
LINDY BOGGS, 1916
NEIL SEDAKA, 1939

March 14

If you would live a happy life, tie it
to a goal, not to people or things.

ALBERT EINSTEIN, 1879

FRANK BORMAN, 1928

QUINCY JONES, 1933

MICHAEL CAINE, 1933

BILLY CRYSTAL, 1947

March 15

ANDREW JACKSON, 1767
HARRY JAMES, 1916
RUTH BADER GINSBURG, 1933
JUDD HIRSCH, 1935

March 16

PAT NIXON, 1912
OSCAR G. MAYER, 1914

There is nothing more
energetic and passionate than being
productive in what you love to do.

JERRY LEWIS, 1926

March 16

DANIEL P. MOYNIHAN, 1927
JERRY JEFF WALKER, 1942
KATE NELLIGAN, 1951

March 17

KATE GREENAWAY, 1846
MERCEDES McCAMBRIDGE, 1918
NAT KING COLE, 1919

March 17

[Dancing] needs commitment
and passion; . . . So much effort for
so little reward—not from the
public and critics, I mean, or the
box office, but from yourself.

RUDOLF NUREYEV, 1938

March 17

KURT RUSSELL, 1951
LESLIE-ANN DOWN, 1954
ROB LOWE, 1964

March 18

EDWARD EVERETT HORTON, 1886

GEORGE PLIMPTON, 1927

JOHN UPDIKE, 1932

WILSON PICKETT, 1941

IRENE CARA, 1959

VANESSA WILLIAMS, 1963

I don't think winning means anything in particular. It's the satisfaction you get from knowing you did your best.

BONNIE BLAIR, 1964

March 19

WYATT EARP, 1848

I'm very pleased with each
advancing year. It stems back to
when I was forty. I was a bit upset
about reaching that milestone, but
an older friend consoled me.
"Don't complain about growing
old—many people don't have
that privilege."

EARL WARREN, 1891

March 19

JOHN J. SIRICA, 1904

PHILIP ROTH, 1933

LYNDA BIRD JOHNSON ROBB, 1944

GLENN CLOSE, 1947

BRUCE WILLIS, 1955

March 20

CARL REINER, 1922

FRED M. ROGERS, 1928

JERRY REED, 1937

PAT RILEY, 1945

BOBBY ORR, 1948

WILLIAM HURT, 1950

SPIKE LEE, 1957

HOLLY HUNTER, 1958

March 21

JOHANN SEBASTIAN BACH, 1685

Our birthdays are feathers in the
broad wing of time.
JEAN PAUL RICHTER, 1763

JOHN D. ROCKEFELLER III, 1906
TIMOTHY DALTON, 1944
MATTHEW BRODERICK, 1962

March 22

CHICO MARX, 1887
LOUIS L'AMOUR, 1908
MARCEL MARCEAU, 1923

PAT ROBERTSON, 1930
WILLIAM SHATNER, 1931
GEORGE BENSON, 1943
ANDREW LLOYD WEBBER, 1948

March 23

FANNIE FARMER, 1857

JOAN CRAWFORD, 1908

ROGER BANNISTER, 1929

MAYNARD JACKSON, 1938

CHAKA KHAN, 1953

March 24

WILLIAM MORRIS, 1834

ANDREW MELLON, 1855

HARRY HOUDINI, 1874

STEVE MCQUEEN, 1930

March 25

ARTURO TOSCANINI, 1867
HOWARD COSELL, 1920
SIMONE SIGNORET, 1921
FLANNERY O'CONNOR, 1925

At 50, the map of how to be a
woman ends. Sixty is much better.
By then you realize there's
something else—a free,
uncharted country.

GLORIA STEINEM, 1934

March 25

ARETHA FRANKLIN, 1942
ELTON JOHN, 1947
SARAH JESSICA PARKER, 1965

March 26

CONDÉ NAST, 1874

ROBERT FROST, 1874

TENNESSEE WILLIAMS, 1911

SANDRA DAY O'CONNOR, 1930

March 26

It's life, Captain,
but not life as we know it.

LEONARD NIMOY, 1931
*as Mr. Spock, in Star Trek:
The Motion Picture*

Learning to believe in yourself
is a lifetime project.

DIANA ROSS, 1944

VICKI LAWRENCE, 1949

March 27

EDWARD STEICHEN, 1879

GLORIA SWANSON, 1899

SARAH VAUGHAN, 1924

DAVID JANSSEN, 1931

CALE YARBOROUGH, 1939

MICHAEL YORK, 1942

March 28

HERBERT H. LEHMAN, 1878
EDMUND MUSKIE, 1914
DIRK BOGARDE, 1921
KEN HOWARD, 1944
DIANE WIEST, 1948

Keep your ducks in a row
at all times. Make every day like
it's your last.

REBA MCENTIRE, 1954

March 29

CY YOUNG, 1867

Oh! Life is so full and rich.
PEARL BAILEY, 1918

EILEEN HECKART, 1919
VANGELIS, 1943

March 30

VINCENT VAN GOGH, 1853
BROOKE ASTOR, 1902
WARREN BEATTY, 1937

March 30

I try to look on every day now
as being a bonus, really . . . life is
very fragile, and that if you are
given another twenty-four hours,
it's a blessing. That's the best way
to look at it.

ERIC CLAPTON, 1945

PAUL REISER, 1957

March 31

JOSEPH HAYDN, 1732
LIZ CLAIBORNE, 1929
JOHN JAKES, 1932
SHIRLEY JONES, 1934

March 31

I like to think that
each of us has his own
little destiny and we have to
seek it—no one will
hand it to us.

RICHARD CHAMBERLAIN, 1935

ALBERT GORE, JR., 1948
RHEA PERLMAN, 1948

Parties, Cakes, Candles, Flowers, and Birthstones

Happy Birthday to You

It should come as no surprise that *Happy Birthday to You* is commonly referred to as "the most frequently sung number in the world." After all, a birthday is one of the few things in life that we all have.

Birthdays mean different things to each of us. When we were children, most of us regarded our birthday with boundless excitement, reveling in our chance to be the focus of attention. To adults, birthdays evoke an enormous range of sentiments, awakening for some of us excitement reminiscent of childhood. Others spend their birthdays reflecting on the events of the passing years or anticipating what the future holds. Yet, no matter how we regard our birthday at a given time, we all feel a certain response to the day. And from time immemorial, one of the very best ways to celebrate a birthday has been to throw a party and have a ball!

Life's a Party

How did birthday parties come to be? The first to throw birthday parties were the ancient Europeans. In those days, people believed strongly in the power of good and evil spirits, and how the evil spirits might prey on a birthday celebrant was unknown. Family and friends would gather 'round the celebrant in order to ward off any evil spirits. Thus, the origins of the first birthday party, replete with good wishes and cheer, were thought to be to protect the celebrant from any mysterious dangers a birthday might present.

Birthday gifts were believed to offer even greater protection from evil spirits. People also reveled in games and fun as a symbol of bidding farewell to the past year and bringing in the new year with joy. In the earliest days, birthday parties were planned for only the most prominent in the community. As time evolved, the custom was shared by common people and eventually children's birthdays became the most celebrated of all. So, birthday parties were first fashioned in order to assure the next year's good fortune.

Have Your Cake and Eat It, Too!

Who first cooked up the idea of a birthday cake? The ancient Greeks believed in Artemis, Goddess of the Moon. In celebration of her birthday, they would bring round, moon-shaped cakes to her temple. Birthday cakes are often round, reminiscent of this custom. In the United States, there has evolved another tradition—that of having the celebrant cut the first slice.

Don't Burn the Candle at Both Ends!

Why the old flame at your birthday party? The first to use lighted candles on birthday cakes were the Germans. The birthday celebrant silently made a wish and then blew out the flames. The wish would be granted only if all the candles were blown out in one puff. The custom to have one candle for each year evolved from this tradition, and in the United States and elsewhere, one candle "to grow on" has been added.

Older Grown

The days are gone,
The months have flown,
And you and I are older grown.
Shake hands, good-bye,
and have no fear
To welcome well another year.

KATE GREENAWAY

Say It with Flowers!

*Each month has a special flower
associated with it.*

Month	Flower
JANUARY	CARNATION
FEBRUARY	PRIMROSE
MARCH	DAFFODIL
APRIL	DAISY
MAY	LILY OF THE VALLEY
JUNE	ROSE
JULY	LARKSPUR
AUGUST	GLADIOLUS
SEPTEMBER	ASTER
OCTOBER	DAHLIA
NOVEMBER	CHRYSANTHEMUM
DECEMBER	POINSETTIA

You're a Gem!

The most widely embraced of the customs associated with birthdays is the wearing of the birthstone—the gemstone which symbolizes the month of your birth. In ancient times, people believed that good luck would be brought to a person wearing his or her birthstone. Many also believed that wearing one's birthstone strengthened character. The following lists the gems generally accepted as the birthstone for each month.

Month	Stone
JANUARY	GARNET
FEBRUARY	AMETHYST
MARCH	AQUAMARINE
APRIL	DIAMOND
MAY	EMERALD
JUNE	PEARL
JULY	RUBY
AUGUST	PERIDOT
SEPTEMBER	SAPPHIRE
OCTOBER	TOURMALINE/OPAL
NOVEMBER	TOPAZ
DECEMBER	TURQUOISE/ZIRCON

Happy
Birthday
to You!

March 4

CHARLES GOREN, 1901

MIRIAM MAKEBA, 1932

JANE GOODALL, 1934

MARY WILSON, 1944

March 5

Those who experience
great unhappiness have an added
capacity for enjoying and being
grateful for happiness
when it comes.

REX HARRISON, 1908

DEAN STOCKWELL, 1936

PENN JILLETTE, 1955

COMPACTS are very different from every other type of adventure game book. They have been specially designed so that their play is as convenient as possible.

The special fold-out flap at the front of the book has all your *game accessories*. Within the fold-out flap at the back are all your *score cards*. This means that whenever you have to amend your score card, it can always be located immediately.

The only thing you have to provide yourself is a pen or pencil. You don't even need an eraser because there are enough score cards (a whole 30!) to allow for a fresh one to be used for each new game.

COMPACTS are ideal for playing at home, on holiday, in the car . . . . wherever you like!

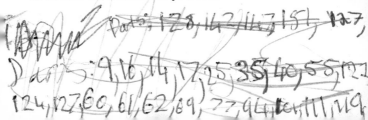

FOOTSTEPS IN THE FOG

Illustrated by Peter Dennis

HODDER AND STOUGHTON
LONDON SYDNEY AUCKLAND

British Library Cataloguing in Publication Data

A catalogue record for this book is available from the British Library

ISBN 0 340 60678 9

Published by Hodder and Stoughton Children's Books,
a division of Hodder Headline plc,
338 Euston Road, London NW1 3BH

Photoset by Rowland Phototypesetting Ltd,
Bury St Edmunds, Suffolk

Printed and bound in Great Britain by
BPCC Hazell Books Ltd
Member of BPCC Ltd

◇ YOUR SINISTER CASE ◇

All week you've been despondently staring out at the grim London houses through the sooty window. What an utter disappointment this job has proved! You wish you had never seen that stupid advertisement!

You felt such a thrill when your eyes had first fallen upon it. The advertisement was in the 16th November 1895 issue of *The Times* and read: *PRIVATE DE-TECTIVE SEEKS YOUNG ASSISTANT. CALL AT 221 BAKER STREET FOR INTERVIEW.*

You could hardly believe your luck. You had always wanted to work with a private detective. And it looked as if you could be working with the best private detective of all. *221 Baker Street* – wasn't that where the famous Sherlock Holmes lived?

Well, yes he did. But at 221*B* Baker Street. Enquiring of the housekeeper there, you were to find that the advertisement was actually placed by the resident downstairs – a Mr Sidney Meek at 221*A*!

Just as ineffectual-looking as his name suggested, Mr Meek was obviously a great admirer of Sherlock Holmes too. In fact, that was precisely why he had moved here. He wanted to emulate his hero and become a world-famous sleuth himself!

For some reason, you eventually allowed him to persuade you to join him in this ambition. It was not quite like working for Sherlock Holmes but you never knew . . . perhaps under that dithery exterior there lurked a brilliant mind.

A whole week has passed now, though, and not one client has called. Every person you've seen enter your building has insisted on being shown straight upstairs to Mr Meek's famous rival.

You're just about to hand in your resignation, however, when you and Mr Meek hear someone pacing up and down just outside your door. They sound like very desperate paces . . . 'Sidney Meek, private detective,' your employer eagerly introduces himself after he has flung open the door. 'Can I be of service?'

'Well, I had rather hoped to speak to Mr Holmes,' the troubled-looking man replies as he dubiously looks Mr Meek up and down. 'But he's out all day on another case, apparently. I just don't know what to do because this is a matter of the utmost importance!'

Mr Meek shoots you an excited glance but he pretends to remain composed as he gently ushers the man towards an armchair. 'Now, let's start from the beginning, shall we?' he invites the stranger calmly. 'And then we'll see if my agency can help.'

'It's to do with this spate of political assassinations,' the man says breathlessly. 'The *"Twenty-seventh Assassinations"* as they're being called, because they've always been on the twenty-seventh of the month. On the twenty-seventh of August it was the Navy minister who was assassinated, on the twenty-seventh of September the Army minister and on the twenty-seventh of October the foreign minister. I'm sure you have closely followed these terrible incidents in the papers.'

'Well, of course,' Mr Meek says. But he quickly

urges the man to continue before he can be tested on this. The truth is that your employer doesn't really like reading papers – and he likes politics even less!

'Well, I think I know who's responsible for the assassinations,' the man says. 'As you know, the papers are saying it's the government of Ruvania – Britain's old enemy. Maybe that evil regime *is* behind it all. But the person who is actually carrying out the murders is, I'm sure, none other than Lord Flaxby.'

'Lord Flaxby!' Mr Meek exclaims, clearly trying to hide the fact that he has never heard of him. 'But his is a name that commands only the highest respect!'

'Yes, I know,' the man admits. 'But I've had occasion to know a very different Gerald Flaxby. It was when we were at university together, some twenty years ago. I was his companion on a small expedition to the Amazonian jungle. The resentful way he talked about his country *then* didn't make him sound so patriotic!'

'You're going to need more evidence against him than that to prove that he's the assassin,' Mr Meek remarks, adopting the sort of casual tone that he is sure his hero upstairs would use.

'Yes, and I'm certain I have it,' the man says gravely. 'You remember reading how each minister was assassinated by a tiny dart tipped with a mysterious poison? The poison made each of the victims' eyeballs turn a strange and horrible green colour. The medical experts were completely baffled by it.'

'Er . . . yes, I'm sure I do remember reading that.'

'Well, we encountered such a poison during our

expedition. A tribe of rainforest pygmies used it to catch their prey. They extracted the poison from a rare pod which grew there and tipped their blow darts with it.'

'And you think Lord Flaxby has been employing this method?' Mr Meek asks with growing excitement.

'He was certainly very fascinated by the poison. He kept joking that if you took a few of the pods back to Europe you could secretly eliminate all your enemies! All it needed, he said, was a more discreet means of firing the poisonous darts. He said the pygmies' long blowpipes were far too obvious.'

'So I wonder what ingenious device he has come up with,' Mr Meek considers thoughtfully. 'Perhaps he has some sort of firing mechanism built into his shoe?'

'No, my guess is that it's his cane. A cane is very like a long blowpipe after all. Perhaps there's a small spring built into his cane which ejects a poisoned dart whenever he presses a secret button. The button could be concealed within the cane's silver top.'

'That's just what I was going to suggest!' Mr Meek breaks in hurriedly, as if he hadn't mentioned that stupid shoe idea at all. 'Yes, the darts are almost certainly fired from Lord Flaxby's cane!' He suddenly acts as if to appear very composed again, though, pressing his fingertips together. 'That's if the assassin *is* Lord Flaxby, of course,' he adds calmly. 'I still say your evidence against him isn't very substantial. Do you have any more?'

'Yes, I've been doing a bit of research. Flaxby's estate is near Cambridge but on the day of each of the assassinations he took the afternoon train down to London. It's far too much of a coincidence.'

'Yes, it is, isn't it!' Mr Meek exclaims, unable to stop his excitement flooding back. It seems that his agency has a case at last! The trouble is . . . he's not quite sure what to do about it. 'So why are you looking for a private detective?' he asks. 'Because you'd like even more research carried out – by experts this time?'

The man jumps to his feet. 'No, there's no time for any of that!' he exclaims desperately. 'Don't you realise – it's the twenty-seventh again today? The twenty-seventh of November! If my suspicions about Flaxby are right, then he should be arriving in London to carry out his next assassination this very afternoon! The reason I'm looking for a private detective is that I want someone to stop him!'

'I see . . .' Mr Meek says slowly, gulping a little. 'So you want us to go and wait for Lord Flaxby's train and secretly follow him across London? Even though he might be very d-dangerous?' he adds with a stammer.

'Yes – that's why I daren't follow Flaxby myself. He'll probably be carrying a whole pocketful of poisoned darts, which he won't hesitate to use on anyone he spots following him. But I gather you sort of people are very used to this tracking business, knowing how to keep well hidden. So you will take up this case, won't you? Another man's life could depend on it. Maybe even the welfare of the whole country!'

◇ GAME INSTRUCTIONS ◇

1. For each attempt at the game, you must use one of the 30 score cards on the fold-out flap at the *back* of the book.
2. The ☠ column on your score card is for showing the *number of poisoned darts that have been fired at you*, the ✐ column the *number of pieces of evidence you have collected against Lord Flaxby* and the 🐟 column which *accessories* you have collected during the game.

☠ Column

3. If a poisoned dart is fired at you during the game, you must mark this on your score card. You do this by deleting the **1** in the ☠ column. If another poisoned dart is fired at you, delete the **2** . . . and another, the **3**.
4. These darts will be near misses but this is as far as your luck goes. The next poisoned dart fired at you – the fourth – will actually strike you. So as soon as you have to delete the **4** in the ☠ column, you must immediately stop the game. If you would like another attempt at it, you must start all over again from the beginning (using a fresh score card).

✐ Column

5. The object of the game is not only to avoid too many darts being fired at you and therefore reach the end of the story, but also to collect as much evidence as

◇ GAME INSTRUCTIONS ◇

possible against Lord Flaxby. At some point while
you are tracking him he might, for example, drop
something that is *proof* that he's working for the
government of Ruvania.

6. Each time you acquire a piece of evidence like this
   you must record it in the 🔎 column. For your first
   piece of evidence circle the **1** in the 🔎 column, for
   the second circle the **2**, and so on.

7. The more times you attempt the game, the better
   your final *pieces of evidence* score should be. Only
   when you have collected the maximum of **6** pieces
   of evidence in one game do you have enough to
   bring Lord Flaxby to justice!

🐾 Column

8. There are three useful *accessories* to be picked up
   during the game: a Map; a Notepad (describing
   Lord Flaxby's special characteristics); and a
   Sketchbook (showing Lord Flaxby's eight accomplices). These three accessories are depicted on
   the fold-out flap at the *front* of the book. Possession
   of the accessories will greatly improve your chances
   of successfully tracking Lord Flaxby and so you
   should make every effort to find them during the
   game.

9. If you *do* pick up one of the accessories, show this
   on your score card by circling that accessory's
   initial (M = Map, N = Notepad, S = Sketchbook)

◇ GAME INSTRUCTIONS ◇

in the 🦀 column. This means that you are then entitled to consult this particular accessory where appropriate during the game.

10. Any accessory not circled in your score card must NOT be consulted at any point during the game.

*To start this dangerous
investigation, turn the page . . .*

Mr Meek hurriedly dons his hat and cloak (which look remarkably like those worn, you've heard, by Sherlock Holmes!). Then, after snatching up a pocket compass, he rushes out into the street. 'Quickly, quickly!' he calls to you. 'We must get to the railway station before Flaxby's train does. It's Liverpool Street station, isn't it, for the Cambridge trains? Now, can you see any cabs?' Well, unfortunately, you *can't*. Not only is dusk starting to fall but quite a thick fog has gathered. The eerie grey swirls mean you can only just see to the opposite pavement. All you can make out by looking to left or right along the street is the faint glow of the street lamps. Suddenly, though, a smaller light appears amongst those yellow glows to the left, accompanied by the sound of horses' hooves. It's a hansom cab approaching! But, as luck would have it, a cab now approaches from the other direction as well . . .

Which cab will you hail?
   If cab coming from left   **go to 27**
   If cab coming from right   **go to 90**

2

'How can it be the one on the left?' Mr Meek asks as he squints through his spectacles in the direction of that man. 'You're not being very observant. A good detective would have noticed the flowers he's holding. What does that tell you about the man? That the person he's waiting to meet is his sweetheart!' Well, in fact, you *had* noticed the flowers but you tell Mr Meek that you're sure he's just carrying them so he doesn't look suspicious as he loiters on the bridge. 'Oh, I didn't think of that,' Mr Meek admits, looking rather embarrassed. 'Yes, you could well be right. Let's start following that man then, because he's now moving away!' *Go to 107.*

3

Full of despair, you and Mr Meek are just about to begin the long trek back to Baker Street when a flower-girl comes walking past. 'Just been nearly knocked over by the rudest man I ever met,' she grumbles. 'Him a gent and all with his fancy top-hat and cane. He was really shouting at me 'e was, demanding to know the way to Grimble's, the apothecary's.' You and Mr Meek suddenly look at each other with hope rising again. Could this have been Lord Flaxby? *Go to 149.*

4

You had noticed Flaxby just in time because you and Mr Meek are able to duck the dart as it comes, hissing through the air towards you. 'Quick!' you shout to Mr Meek, pushing him towards the road. 'Let's hurry towards that cab before he can reload!' You both leap inside the cab, ordering the driver to take you quickly to the other side of Parliament Square. To your relief, you don't notice Flaxby running out of the fog after you. But when your cabbie brings you back towards Big Ben, you see that he has completely vanished again! *Go to 58.*

5

The first two sets of footsteps you hear approaching from the coffee house are quite easy to discount. They're obviously women's. But what about this third set which is now slowly coming towards your hiding-place? They're clearly a *man's* footsteps – but are they Flaxby's? They sound so sinister that you daren't look as the dark figure passes your doorway. You press yourselves right into the corner to avoid any risk of being spotted. It's only when the man is some way past

that you creep right out and take a long look at him. 'Should we follow him or not?' you ask uncertainly as you both peer at the man's receding back.

If you have circled the N in your score card's  column, you may consult the NOTEPAD accessory now to help work out whether this is Flaxby. If not, you'll have to take a risk:

    If follow the man   go to 130
    If continue to wait   go to 21

6

You both crouch right down behind the cart, so you're able to see Flaxby's feet as he talks to the passer-by. If he suddenly heads back in this direction, you want as much warning as possible! 'I think he's asking the other person directions for Tower Bridge,' Mr Meek whispers as you both try to hear their exchange. 'And he isn't very polite about it either. I've never heard such an unpleasant tone of—hey, what's that that's dropped from the folds of his cloak?' he interrupts himself suddenly. 'It's a little book of some sort. When he starts walking again, we'll sneak out and pick it up!' *Go to 156.*

7

Unfortunately, you can't quite hear what the two men are saying to each other from this distance. You daren't move any closer in case the fog no longer provides sufficient cover. The meeting proves very short and you and Mr Meek both hold your breath as the two men now prepare to go their different ways. To your immense relief, neither of them comes in your direction! You discreetly start following Flaxby's hazy silhouette . . . but he hasn't walked very far when he's accosted by that beggar! *Go to 95.*

8

Travelling in an easterly direction from Tower Bridge, you find yourselves in a particularly gloomy part of London. There seems to be nothing here except dark warehouses and sinister alleys. 'This can't be right,' Mr Meek remarks. 'I can't imagine finding a library in this grim quarter. I'll ask the cabbie to stop and try a westerly direction. Without delay!' he exclaims with a shiver in his voice. *Go to 132.*

9

'Don't run too fast,' Mr Meek warns you as you both chase after the man's disappearing silhouette. 'We don't want him to hear us!' His warning comes too late, though, because it looks as if the man *has* heard you. He suddenly stops dead in his tracks and turns round. 'Excuse me, do either of you have the time?' he asks innocently. So it isn't Lord Flaxby, after all . . . this man's face is quite different! You both now hare back towards the other man. There's absolutely no doubt that this one *is* Flaxby. For, just as you spot him in the distance, he suddenly turns round and fires one of his deadly darts at you. It only just misses your shoulder!

Delete the top number in your score card's ☠ column to record this narrow miss. Go next to 89.

10

'Are you all right?' Mr Meek cries with concern as he sees you fall to the floor. 'That demon hasn't hit you, has he?' You give your employer a reassuring grin, though, using his arm to pull yourself up again. 'No, I was just *pretending* to be hit,' you tell him, 'so he didn't fire a second dart. And the ploy worked, too, because – look – he's run off somewhere. It's probably right out of the library so he can continue his journey. We'd better hurry before we lose him!' ***Go to 114.***

11

You and Mr Meek search one aisle after another on the ground floor, cautiously peering along each of the long rows of books. 'He must be on one of the floors above,' Mr Meek remarks after this search proves unsuccessful. 'Let's keep an eye on the stairway over there and wait for him to come down. We'll hide behind this tall bookcase so he doesn't see us. I'll just remove a couple of the books to make a secret viewing hole!' *Go to 97*.

12

'I wonder why Flaxby wanted to call at an apothecary's?' you ask as the pair of you continue secretly to watch him in the little shop opposite. 'Perhaps to buy some more deadly poison just in case his special type runs out,' Mr Meek suggests quietly. 'Or perhaps to buy an antidote in case he accidentally touches a trace of his poison himself! He's certainly purchasing *some* sort of potion there because – look! – the apothecary has just

handed him a small bottle.' There's no time for you to
focus on this bottle, though, because Flaxby then
almost immediately emerges from the shop. You and
Mr Meek quickly retreat deep into the shadows of the
doorway . . . *Go to 148.*

13

Your choice was a wise one. For as you're both running
towards the queue for the hansom cab, Mr Meek
suddenly pulls you back. 'There's Lord Flaxby!' he
whispers excitedly. 'You see? Eighth from the front in
the queue. He's quite tall and the bottom part of his left
ear is missing – just like our client described him!' You
ask Mr Meek whether you should immediately join the
cab queue yourselves but he shakes his head. 'No, we'll
observe him secretly from here for a while,' he replies,
'and jot down a few of his details and habits while we
wait. This information will make it easier to identify
him again should we lose him during our pursuit!' *Go
to 141.*

14

You and Mr Meek hide behind one of the old cannons in front of the Tower so you can secretly watch the man as he waits at Traitor's Gate. 'Come on, Flaxby, where are you?' you mutter tensely to yourself. A moment later, you receive your answer – in the form of a dart which comes hissing through the air and only just misses your head! Quickly swinging round, you see that Flaxby's silhouette is actually *behind* you, and he's looking down on you from Tower Bridge. It must have been one of those other two loiterers he was meeting, and he must have spotted you crouching down behind the cannon!

Delete the top number in your score card's ☠ ***column to record this near miss. Go next to 26.***

15

'What do we do now?' you ask Mr Meek with concern. 'Flaxby's probably lost us completely by now!' Your eccentric employer doesn't answer, though, leaving you standing there while he wanders inside the little tavern. But several minutes later, you discover that he *isn't* so eccentric. 'I asked in there if anyone noticed Flaxby,' he tells you excitedly. 'One woman did. She said he sat on his own at a small table in the corner, taking a seat just vacated by a man in a cloth cap. It made me wonder if this man had left something for Flaxby on that table. My suspicion was right. I found this beer-mat where Flaxby had been sitting . . . and with some tiny instructions pencilled on the other side!' *Go next to 146.*

16

'I'm sure that beggar's cap he's holding is just so that Flaxby will be able to identify him!' you whisper to Mr Meek as you both focus on this man in the centre. 'Look, he's starting to walk towards us. Perhaps our silhouettes look even hazier than his does and he's mistaken one of us for Flaxby!' As the man comes closer, though, you begin to wonder whether it is *you* who has made the mistake. 'Spare an odd copper, mates?' the man now calls out to you through the fog. 'Hey, look out!' he yells suddenly. 'There's this shadowy figure standing under that lamp way over there and I think he's about to fire something at you!'

Delete the top number in your score card's 💀 *column to record this attempt on your life. Go to 48.*

17

As your cab rumbles off in a westerly direction, you both lean right forward so you can help your cabbie spot Lamp Street Library. A few roads further on, you suddenly feel strangely uncomfortable. It's as you're about to pass a stationary cab. The driver is wearing a bright yellow muffler. That's what Flaxby's driver was wearing! Did Flaxby order his cabbie to stop a while in case you managed to pick up his route? But you realise all this too late – because a dart suddenly comes whistling towards you from inside that other cab. Will you be able to duck in time?

Delete the top number in your score card's ☠ column to record this attempt on your life. If you survive it, go to 132.

18

You and Mr Meek both lean right over the stone balcony of the gallery, studying each person that passes underneath. For quite a while you see no one that looks even remotely like Flaxby – but then someone comes into view who *could* possibly be him. 'The trouble is,

we've never seen Flaxby with his hat off before,'
Mr Meek says softly as you both peer down on the man.
'So we don't know whether he has that style of hair or

not! I know it's a very difficult angle from up here, but is
there any other feature about this man which might
suggest he's Flaxby?'

If you have circled the N in your score card's
*column, you may consult the NOTEPAD accessory
now to help work out whether this is Flaxby. If not,
you'll have to take a risk:*

    If keep watching man   **go to 117**
    If disregard him   **go to 64**

19

The bootmaker's doorway is on the same side of the
road as the coffee house – but twenty metres or so to the
left of it. 'A good choice!' Mr Meek compliments you

after you have crossed over to it and hidden yourselves within its shadows. 'We're just close enough to be able to *hear* people as they come out of the coffee house. If they walk off in the other direction, we can peep out and see what they look like from behind. If they come this way, we can get a good look as they pass!' *Go to 5.*

20

You've walked about a quarter of a mile in this southerly direction when you hear an eerie tapping coming from the fog in front of you. But then a voice suddenly calls out to reassure you. 'I'm nothing to be afraid of,' the voice says, chuckling. 'It's just me—Blind Ben, the match-seller. Although in this thick fog, I'm probably no more blind than you are! I can hear from your hesitant steps that you're uncertain of your way. Let me direct you. I might be blind but I know every single street and house in London!' This proves not to be an idle boast either. When you ask him the directions for Grimble's, the apothecary's, he's able to give them to you immediately. Unfortunately, though, you have been going the wrong way! *Go to 77.*

21

'I hope we haven't made the wrong decision in choosing to wait,' Mr Meek says, growing more and more twitchy as the minutes pass. 'If the man that walked by just then *was* Flaxby, we'll never catch him up again!' And more and more it appears that you *did* make the wrong decision. For no one else in top-hat and cape steps out of the coffee house. 'It looks as though it *was* Flaxby that passed us!' Mr Meek says in a panic. 'Quick – as fast as we can!' he exclaims, starting to run in the direction in which Flaxby has disappeared. 'We'll just have to hope that he isn't walking too fast!' ***Go to 142.***

22

You continue to follow the sound of Flaxby's footsteps along the dark and deserted streets – but then that sound suddenly disappears! You both rush down a long street, frantically searching for him through the fog. 'He must have popped into one of those gloomy little shops back there,' Mr Meek says, panting, when you reach the very end of the street. 'Rather than go and search every one of them, let's make our way to Tower Bridge ahead of Flaxby. We'll just have to hope we meet up with him again *there!* **Go to 118.**

23

'We won't move just yet,' Mr Meek whispers, shivering with excitement. 'We'll pretend to be interested in this shelf of books here until he's gone down past this floor. Then we'll secretly follow him down to the ground floor!' **Go to 68.**

24

As soon as you've taken your seats, however, you suddenly remember to look at the man's left ear. It's perfectly normal . . . so it's not Flaxby after all! He must be somewhere in the circle then,' you remark with frustration, lifting your head. 'What a nuisance we can't see the circle audience, sitting here.' What you *can* see as you move your head around, though, are the private boxes on either side of the music hall. You can't see into

them too well because they're quite shadowy inside, but from the shadows of a box up to your right a pair of hands suddenly appears, resting on the ledge. Do they belong to Flaxby?

If you have circled the N in your score card's column, you may consult the NOTEPAD accessory now to help work out whether this is Flaxby. If not, you'll have to take a risk:

> *If assume it is*   **go to 121**
> *If assume it isn't*   **go to 57**

25

'There's Lord Flaxby's cab – the one we're just about to overtake!' Mr Meek exclaims, hurriedly leaning forwards. 'I memorised its number at the station – 8665!' You both peer intently across at the other cab, hoping to obtain a glimpse of Lord Flaxby. But he's sitting well back. You're just asking Mr Meek if he's absolutely sure that was the number of Flaxby's cab when a black pole suddenly protrudes from its open front. It must be Flaxby's cane because a moment later a dart comes whistling into your cab, narrowly missing your head! 'He must have recognised us from the station and guessed that we were following him!' you say, gasping, as Flaxby's cab now accelerates past you again and quickly disappears round a corner.

Delete the top number in your score card's ☠ *column to record this narrow escape of yours. Go next to 34.*

26

Fortunately, Flaxby seems in a hurry to continue his journey. After a quick exchange with his accomplice, he leaps into the first hansom cab that comes clattering on to the bridge. Of course, it's not *that* fortunate, because unless you can quickly hail a cab yourselves, you've lost him! Luckily, a second cab appears very soon afterwards and Mr Meek urgently orders the driver to follow Flaxby's vehicle. The cabbie is just cracking his whip over his horse, however, when an alarm bell rings. Tower Bridge is starting to open! 'Blow, he's got away!' Mr Meek cries with anguish as Flaxby's cab now disappears out of sight on the far side of the river. ***Go to 103.***

27

'Cabbie!' you yell into the fog as the sound of the horse's hooves approaching from the left grow louder. You stand right at the edge of the pavement to try to help him see you. But it looks as if he's going to continue blindly past because the hooves keep clattering on the other side of the road. Suddenly they stop, however, and the cabbie brings his vehicle towards you and Mr Meek. 'Where to, Mister?' he calls down to your employer. 'What's that you say – Liverpool Street railway station?' he shouts through his muffler. 'OK, climb into me cab. But don't expect any records in this fog!' ***Go to 66.***

28

As your hansom cab sets off in a southerly direction, rattling slowly through the fog, Mr Meek keeps muttering anxiously to himself. 'Oh, why didn't we just push right to the front of that queue and grab the cab immediately after Lord Flaxby's?' he asks in frustration. 'I bet that's the last we ever see of the scoundrel!' His glum face has just glanced up again, though, when it suddenly brightens. 'Gosh, there's his cab right in front of us!' he exclaims. 'I memorised its number back at the railway station!' You only manage to tail Flaxby's cab for a short distance, however. For it suddenly speeds off into the fog. It looks as if Flaxby has guessed that he is being followed! *Go to 34.*

29

'Look at this strange coin that fell from the bottom of Flaxby's trouser-leg while he was running down the stairway,' you tell your employer as you bend down to pick it up. 'He must have a small hole in his pocket. Ah, so that's why it looks so strange. It's Ruvanian! And it's in mint condition, so Flaxby's fingerprints might well be the only ones on it. This is surely quite strong evidence against him!'

Well done. Record this piece of vital evidence collected in your score card's ♺ column. Go next to 114.

30

Approaching the Victoria Tower end of the Houses of Parliament, you notice a small red glow through the fog. You suddenly hold Mr Meek back as you realise

that it's a chestnut-seller's glowing brazier. 'Perhaps he isn't a real chestnut-seller,' you whisper tensely, 'but just Flaxby's contact in disguise! Or if it's not him that's the contact, it might be that customer he's just serving. There's a good chance that it's *one* of those two. I certainly can't see anyone else loitering around here at the moment!'

If you have circled the S in your score card's  *column, you may consult the SKETCHBOOK accessory now to find out which of these two is Flaxby's contact. If not, you'll have to guess:*

   If chestnut-seller   go to 98
   If his customer   go to 62

31

You and Mr Meek tensely glance at each other as the man who was reading the Bible slowly rises from the pew. 'Look, he's walking towards the collection box at the other end of the nave,' your employer whispers, nervously adjusting his glasses. 'Perhaps that's his arranged meeting place with Flaxby. Let's creep a little closer to the collection box so – assuming my theory is right – we can hear what the two men have to say to each other!' *Go to 144.*

32

Luckily, the dart hisses through the air just to the right of your ear . . . but you can see Flaxby hurriedly starting to reload his cane. You frantically rush towards his hazy figure to try to prevent him. For a moment, it looks as if you're not going to be in time but then he suddenly fumbles with his cane and drops it on the ground. You hear a loud curse, but as soon as he's picked the cane up again, he runs off, disappearing into the night. *Go next to 123.*

33

You'd both completely forgotten that Flaxby had a cab waiting for him outside the music hall. As a result, he's able to get away much more quickly than you'd anticipated. He's already speeding away into the fog as you and Mr Meek rush out of the building. 'This time we definitely have lost him for good!' Mr Meek cries in despair after looking around in vain for another cab. 'Not only will we never be able to catch him up now but we don't even know where he's going!' But then you hear a quiet chuckle behind you. 'You might not know where he's going, guv,' a friendly voice says, 'but Bert Hayes does!' Turning round, you see that it's the cabbie who dropped you off here. ***Go to 115.***

34

At least you now know that you must be heading in the right direction for Garrick's Coffee House and, sure enough, you eventually spot the warm glow of its windows on a street corner. You and Mr Meek are very tense as you step down from your cab, worried that Flaxby might be secretly watching you from the shadows of one of the nearby doorways. But it seems that you are safe for the moment. 'Flaxby must be inside the coffee house,' Mr Meek says, breathing a sigh of relief. 'I dare say he's chatting with one of his London friends so it looks as if his journey down here is perfectly innocent! We'll hide in one of these doorways until he comes out again. Which one do you suggest?'

If barber's doorway   ***go to 126***
If bootmaker's doorway   ***go to 19***
If tobacconist's doorway   ***go to 91***

35

You keep your eyes on this suspect as he continues to survey the audience beneath him. Suddenly, he seems to spot the person he was looking for and you hold your breath as he hurriedly steps down past the rows of seats. He goes right to the front row, just before the balcony rail. You grab Mr Meek's sleeve as he squeezes along this row, sitting next to a man who has Flaxby's same erect back! But then you happen to glance beyond the two men, towards one of the private boxes on the far side of the music hall. Your glance is too late. For the tip of a cane has already extended from the shadows of this box – and it's aimed directly at you!

Delete the top number in your score card's ☠ column to record this attempt on your life. If you survive it, go to 87.

36

Flaxby must have guessed that you and Mr Meek were waiting for him just outside the cathedral. You've been hiding in the fog there for a good twenty minutes now but still he hasn't emerged. Suddenly, though, he rushes out and leaps down the broad steps for the nearest cab. You and Mr Meek frantically search for a cab yourselves but, by the time one arrives, Flaxby's vehicle has well and truly disappeared into the fog. 'Never mind,' you tell your employer, as you both board your cab. 'I think I heard him order his driver to go to Partridge's the Pawnbrokers, wherever that might be. Our own driver will doubtless know.' Unfortunately, though, he doesn't. This is beginning to look quite desperate . . .

If you have circled the M in your score card's 🗞️ *column, you may consult the MAP accessory now to find out the rough direction of Partridge's the Pawnbrokers from St Paul's Cathedral. If not, you'll have to take a risk:*

If order cabbie north	*go to 92*
If order cabbie east	*go to 80*
If order cabbie west	*go to 120*

You and Mr Meek make your way to the library's second floor, climbing the narrow wooden staircase. 'Perhaps you should take your deerstalker off,

Mr Meek?' you suggest tactfully as you start to creep from one aisle of dusty books to another. 'Wearing a hat rather gives you away now that we are indoors!' Mr Meek's mind is clearly somewhere else, however. 'You see those three men on the far side of the room?' he

whispers to you excitedly. 'Each one has anxiously taken out his pocket watch in the last half minute. So they're probably each waiting to meet someone here. And perhaps one of them is waiting to meet Flaxby!'

If you have circled the S in your score card's 🐿 *column, you may consult the SKETCHBOOK accessory now to find out which of these three men you should keep an eye on. If not, you'll have to take a risk:*

Man with folded arms	*go to 128*
Man sitting at table	*go to 75*
Man still checking watch	*go to 56*

38

Bert's horse has been cantering in a westerly direction for a good quarter of an hour now but still you haven't come across the Dirty Duck tavern. 'It's unlikely to be any further west than this,' Mr Meek tells you frantically, 'because that would take us back into the Baker Street area. If there were a Dirty Duck tavern around there, I'm sure I would know about it! Our guess was obviously a wrong one. I'll ask Bert to head straight back for the music hall and try south this time!' ***Go to 55.***

39

You and Mr Meek strain your ears to listen to more of the conversation on the other side of the bookcase. But Mr Meek leans just a bit too close to the books and causes one to fall on its side. You both anxiously hold your breath as the conversation in the next aisle immediately stops. Then you hear hurried footsteps . . . and just glimpse Flaxby fleeing down the staircase. You both run after him but, part of the way down the stairs, you suddenly make Mr Meek stop. ***Go to 29.***

40

You at last reach Partridge's the Pawnbrokers. 'There it is!' you exclaim, just able to make out three brass balls hanging above one of the shops ahead. 'At least, it's definitely a *pawnbroker's*. Let's just hope the name Partridge is above the door!' A moment later, you're able to see that 'Partridge' *is* painted there – and you and Mr Meek hurriedly squeeze through the folding door of your cab. In the excitement of your discovery, however, you'd both neglected to check the other hansom cabs standing in this part of the street. From the dark interior of one of them, the tip of a cane suddenly appears, aimed directly at you . . .

Delete the top number in your score card's 💀 column to record this attempt on your life. If you survive it, go to 145.

41

'Look at this skull and crossbones on the label,' Mr Meek remarks as he picks the bottle up with his handkerchief. 'This must be one of Flaxby's poison bottles! And, unless he was always wearing gloves when he handled it, the surface should be covered with his fingerprints!' So, before you both hurry out of the music hall after Flaxby, Mr Meek wraps his handkerchief very carefully round the bottle and puts it in his pocket. It should be a wonderful piece of evidence!

Well done. Record this piece of vital evidence collected in your score card's ✍ column. Go to 33.

42

You were very lucky that you didn't follow that hazy figure. For, less than a minute later, another person approaches from the north side of the square, disappearing in roughly the same direction. He would have been right behind you if you had followed that first man. It wouldn't have mattered if this second person also wasn't Flaxby, of course, but you notice that the cloaked silhouette taps his cane in a small puddle as he passes. Creeping up to this puddle, you see that the damp cane has left a print just beyond it. The print is in the form not of a solid circle as you would expect, but a thin ring. In other words, the middle of the cane was hollow – just like you know Flaxby's to be! *Go to 123.*

43

'It looks as if he's going inside the cathedral,' Mr Meek whispers to you as you both watch Flaxby leap up the broad steps towards its main entrance. 'He must be meeting someone in there. We'll wait a couple of minutes and then creep inside ourselves.' But Flaxby has well and truly disappeared by the time you two cautiously enter the cathedral. You have absolutely no idea whether he's gone down into the crypt, climbed up into the dome . . . or is still somewhere in the nave!

Where will you search?
 If crypt   go to 135
 If dome   go to 110
 If nave   go to 74

44

'Look!' you exclaim, suddenly grabbing Mr Meek's arm as Flaxby's driver at last flicks his whip over his horse. 'Flaxby's cab is starting to move away. He must have assumed he's finally lost us!' Just in case Flaxby's still a little suspicious, though, and is secretly looking back out of the cab's window, you wait until his vehicle has almost completely disappeared into the fog. Only then do you instruct your own cabbie to start cautiously following . . . *Go to 71.*

45

You both press yourselves well into the doorway, praying that someone doesn't suddenly step out of the building and give you away. You can't see Flaxby from this hiding-place – but you can just about hear him as he speaks to the passer-by. 'Are you deaf, man?' he addresses him gruffly. 'I asked you directions for Tower Bridge, not the Tower of London! Oh, they're very close to each other? Well, why didn't you say so in the first place?' Flaxby now walks away from the poor passer-by and you wait until he's a fair distance ahead of you again before leaving your hiding-place. *Go to 22.*

46

You duck just in time as the lethal dart comes hissing out of Flaxby's raised cane. Before he has time to load a second one, you push Mr Meek back towards the exit and tumble through it with him. 'We'll be a much harder target for him out here in the fog,' you say, panting. 'Of course, he'll probably now decide to stay in the cathedral a good deal longer to try to lose us once more. Let's go round to the main entrance at the front in the hope that that's where he'll eventually slip out.' *Go to 36.*

47

Creeping up to the aisles of tall bookcases, you immediately spot one of those two men. He's standing in the very first aisle. But there's nothing suspicious about him. He's merely reaching up for a book. So you both tiptoe towards the end of the second aisle . . . and then the third. 'The other man is about halfway down that aisle!' Mr Meek exclaims, suddenly pulling you back. 'And he's Flaxby's contact all right! Why am I so sure? Because Flaxby himself was there as well, whispering something into the man's ear. We'll watch for the scoundrel to leave and then secretly hurry after him!' *Go to 114.*

48

You hear Flaxby's dart whistling just above your head as you and Mr Meek both hurl yourselves to the ground. 'Is he still there?' your employer asks, panting nervously, not daring to look up. You very slowly lift your face and peer back at the yellow haze under the streetlamp. The dark silhouette has now left it. 'Flaxby seems to have hurried off somewhere,' you tell Mr Meek as you rise warily to your feet. 'The trouble is, so has his contact waiting at the bottom of Nelson's Column. Look, there's no one there now. So it looks as if we're going to miss the chance of eavesdropping on their conversation!' *Go to 123.*

49

'The dart didn't hit you, did it?' Mr Meek exclaims after you have desperately thrown yourselves to either side of the stairway. You reach just above your shoulder and pluck the evil little spike from the stairway's handrail. 'Not quite!' You smile with relief. But then you quickly rise to your feet, seeing Flaxby's cloak swirl out through the library's exit. 'Come on, Mr Meek!' you implore him. 'The pursuit is on again!' *Go to 114.*

50

'C-can you see him anywhere out there?' Mr Meek stammers as you cautiously peep out from the doorway. You peer into the thick curtain of fog, from one sinister shadow to the next, but you can't detect any movement. Yes, you can! You can just see the silhouette of a man slipping out of one of the shadows and hurriedly making its way towards the other end of the long street. You're sure the man's gently laughing to himself as he goes! Flaxby must have realised that he was being watched from outside the coffee house and as you and Mr Meek started to follow the other man, he secretly followed *you*! *Go to 89.*

51

You're just about to start your long, gloomy trek back to Baker Street when a flower-girl comes walking past. 'Blimey, you fancy-dressed sorts are so rude!' she tells you. 'A couple of minutes ago, this toff all but knocks me and my flowers over, demanding the way to Grimble's, the apothecary's shop. Blooming cheek!' You and Mr Meek swap quick, hopeful glances. Could this have been Lord Flaxby? *Go to 149.*

52

'I do hope your guess is right,' Mr Meek remarks anxiously. 'Look, the man is now closing his paper as if he's about to wander off somewhere. Once we start following him, it'll mean we can't keep an eye on those other two!' *You* hope your guess is right as well because the man starts to leave the bridge altogether. He descends some steps which lead down towards the Tower of London. 'Look, he's following the path which runs in front of the Tower,' Mr Meek says, panting, as you hurriedly start to descend the steps yourselves. 'Wait a minute – he's stopped. Right in front of Traitor's Gate!' *Go to 14.*

You and Mr Meek keep tensely peering up at Big Ben as you wait underneath it. You can just read the clock face through the fog. First, it shows eight twenty . . . then eight thirty . . . then eight thirty-four . . . but there's still no sign of Flaxby. 'It looks as if his rendezvous was at the Victoria Tower end after all!' Mr Meek says with a sigh. 'Wait, though,' he adds excitedly. 'Perhaps he's

the murky figure approaching from that direction right now. Look, the person's stopped to read something. Now's our chance to take a good look at him!'

If you have circled the N in your score card's *column, you may consult the NOTEPAD accessory now to help you work out whether this is Flaxby. If not, you'll have to take a risk:*

If continue to watch figure	*go to 134*
If disregard him	*go to 60*

For a moment you'd both been a sitting target because you didn't have time to move well enough away from the grid. Fortunately, though, Flaxby's dart whistled exactly between you both. It was desperately close . . . but neither of you was hit. 'We're out of range from that grid now, Mr Meek,' you say, gasping, having both moved as fast and as far as you could while Flaxby was reloading. 'Still,' you warn, 'there are several other grids above us in the ceiling. Before Flaxby hurries over to a nearer one, let's leave this crypt. In fact, let's leave this cathedral altogether and wait for Flaxby just outside where we'll be a lot safer!' *Go to 36.*

55

South, fortunately, turns out to be the correct direction for the Dirty Duck. Some half-mile from Old Nell's Music Hall, Bert suddenly spots a tavern light bearing this curious name. 'I hope Flaxby hasn't already left,' Mr Meek says anxiously as Bert quickly draws up opposite the noisy building. 'I can't see his vehicle anywhere . . . can you?' You both leap out of the cab and dash across the road towards the tavern's glowing, misted-up windows. As you're pressing your faces to one window, however, you suddenly hear Bert cry out from behind you. 'Look out!' he yells. 'There's someone lurking in that shadowy doorway over there and he's about to fire something at you!'

Delete the top number in your score card's ☠ *column to record this attempt on your life. If you survive it, go to 104.*

56

The moment the man puts his pocket watch away again, he starts to wander from the table. 'Look, he's disappeared amongst those long aisles of tall bookcases over there,' Mr Meek whispers tensely. 'I think it was the third aisle he went down. We'll tiptoe down the second aisle and listen out for Flaxby's voice. I'm sure it won't be very long before we hear it there!' *Go to 140.*

57

It's very fortunate that you didn't pay too much attention to this box. If you had, you might not have turned your head and spotted the suspicious figure in the box on the other side of the music hall. This figure too is virtually hidden in shadow but, again, you can just make out the hands. They're idly toying with a small bottle – and an evil-looking dart! You quickly pull Mr Meek out of his seat, tugging him behind you right to the very end of the row. You're now almost directly underneath Flaxby's box – and, unless he leans right out of it, quite safe from his lethal weapon. ***Go next to 102.***

58

You and Mr Meek dash one way, then another beneath the foggy silhouette of the Houses of Parliament, anxiously trying to find Flaxby again. This time it's more important than ever because you're absolutely convinced that he's going to attempt the assassination very soon now. It's then that you hear a foghorn sounding on the Thames. Your whole body chills at the sound. Didn't you read in this morning's *Times* that the prime minister would be travelling by steamboat to Greenwich this very afternoon? And that he was due back at the Houses of Parliament just before nine o'clock to make an important speech? 'I have this terrible feeling that it's not just any old minister that Flaxby is planning to assassinate this time,' you tell Mr Meek weakly. 'But the *prime minister*. And unless I'm much mistaken, Flaxby is to carry out that assassination from Westminster Bridge!' **Go to 113.**

59

Deciding you're much more likely to be safe from Flaxby's darts *inside* the library rather than outside it, you and Mr Meek dash back in again. You then hide behind one of the tall bookcases once more and wait until you see Flaxby leave the library. At last you do see him go and, after a short delay, you cautiously step through the exit door yourselves. But you've let Flaxby get a bit *too* far ahead because he's already completely vanished in the fog! **Go to 3.**

60

You chose to disregard this man in front of you because you suddenly noticed another cloaked figure. He hurriedly leaps down from a hansom cab as it races into Parliament Square. Surely this one is much more likely to be Flaxby! But as your eyes cautiously follow the urgent figure, you suddenly notice that the man in front has started moving again. No, he hasn't. He's just quickly aiming his cane at you!

Delete the top number in your score card's ☠ column to record this attempt on your life. If you survive it, go to 4.

61

'I hope this *is* Lord Flaxby we're following,' Mr Meek whispers anxiously as you track the hazy figure right to the end of the street and round a corner. 'If he was that other man, then we've surely lost him for good!' As the dark figure passes under a street lamp, though, you realise that it *isn't* Flaxby. This man wears a monocle, which you can see glinting under the light. You're just starting to hurry back towards the coffee house when you hear a quiet hiss near your ear. 'Quick, leap into this doorway,' you cry, yanking Mr Meek by the arm. 'That was one of Flaxby's poisoned darts!'

Delete the top number in your score card's ☠ column to record this narrow miss. Go next to 50.

62

This suspect now moves away from the chestnut-seller, hurrying across the road towards Westminster Abbey. Keeping at a discreet distance, you and Mr Meek cross the road after him. Just in case you made a mistake about the man, though, you take a last look back at the chestnut-seller. It's a good thing you did! A second man has appeared at the glowing brazier – but he's not buying chestnuts like the first one did. He's aiming his cane at you over the chestnut-seller's shoulder!

Delete the top number in your score card's ☠ *column to record this attempt on your life. If you survive it, go to 79.*

63

Although you both pretend to lower your eyes from the grid, you still keep it secretly in sight. All the time you move fraction by fraction away from it. You were very wise doing this because the tip of a cane is suddenly poked through one of the grid's holes. It's then angrily withdrawn again. You'd both edged just far enough away for Flaxby to realise you're out of his range! *Go next to 88.*

64

It's fortunate that you didn't pay too much attention to that man because he might have drawn your eyes away from a new arrival under your balcony. This man quite definitely is Flaxby! Not only does he pace about very shiftily, but he suddenly glances up at your balcony, offering a full view of his face. So you certainly see *him*. The question is, has he seen *you*? **Go to 93.**

65

You both pray you were right about this man not being Flaxby. But when he has reached the bottom of the stairway, you hear him coming towards the very aisle in which you are hiding! 'You don't think he s-somehow saw us through the g-gap in the books?' Mr Meek asks with chattering teeth. 'You don't think he's got his cane all ready to fire at us?' You'll very soon find out. For the footsteps are about to turn into your aisle . . . **Go next to 139.**

66

The fog becomes thicker and thicker as your hansom cab makes its way to Liverpool Street station . . . and your speed, therefore, gets slower and slower. Mr

Meek keeps tensely checking his pocket watch. 'Flaxby's train will be arriving in just a quarter of an hour,' he says anxiously, 'and we must have at least a mile still to go!' He raps frantically on the cab roof and asks the driver if he can go any faster. 'What, in this pea-souper of a fog? Yer must be joking, mate!' the cabbie shouts back. 'Don't think I've ever seen it so bad. Can barely see me own 'orse, let alone any other on the road!' *Go next to 138.*

67

Your cab has travelled only a little way south of Tower Bridge when it suddenly draws to a halt. 'I wonder why we've stopped,' Mr Meek says. 'Perhaps our driver has spotted Lamp Street Library!' It turns out that he hasn't, unfortunately, but what he has spotted is a policeman. 'I hear you're looking for Lamp Street Library, sir,' the bobby says to Mr Meek, after he has waddled up to the open end of your cab. 'Here – you wouldn't be that famous Sherlock 'olmes, would you? No, of course, you ain't. It was just that hat and cape of yours. But you're much more gawky than what Mr 'olmes is meant to look. Anyway . . . Lamp Street Library? Yer want to turn your cab in a westerly direction!' *Go to 17.*

68

Mr Meek takes several secret glances at the stairway, nervously checking over the top of his glasses, and then he suddenly plucks at your arm. 'He's now descended below this floor!' he exclaims softly. 'Quick! To the stairs ourselves!' You reach the top of this flight of steps just as Flaxby reaches the very bottom. And it definitely *is* Flaxby down there because you see him furtively extract a small bottle from his pocket and check that the top is securely fastened. And you can just make out a skull and crossbones on the bottle! It obviously contains that special poison for his darts! *Go to 114.*

69

Your cab hasn't travelled far in a westerly direction when it suddenly stops. 'Looks like it will have to be one of them other directions,' the driver calls down. 'The fog's caused an almighty pile-up ahead. Try south this time, shall I?' You and Mr Meek become more and more anxious as you rattle down one foggy street after another. Garrick's Coffee House is still nowhere to be found. You've just leant forward to give yourself as good a view as possible of the murky buildings when something comes whistling into your vehicle, narrowly missing your face. 'It's one of Flaxby's poisoned darts!' Mr Meek exclaims as he extracts the evil object from the upholstery. 'He must have realised we were watching him at the station and has been hiding somewhere, waiting for our cab to come along!'

Delete the top number in your score card's  *column to record this near miss. Go next to 34.*

70

While the man to his left and right are still surveying the seats in front of them, this one in the centre suddenly seems to spot the person he has come to meet. He must have spotted him not in the circle, though, but in one of the private boxes at the side of the music hall. For, after peering in that direction, he hurriedly leaves the back of the circle – to make his way round to that box, presumably. You immediately peer towards the boxes yourself. Just visible in one of them is a silhouette, furtively sitting back amongst the shadows. You have no doubt that this is Flaxby! *Go to 99.*

71

For the first half-mile or so your cabbie doggedly
follows Flaxby's vehicle. Then a baker's boy suddenly
steps out in front of the horse, making him swerve
wildly into the pavement. 'Afraid I've lost him, guv!' he
calls down to Mr Meek after he has shouted all sorts of
curses at the boy. 'I can remember the cab's number,
though. What I'll do is keep going, and hope that I see it
stopped somewhere. That's all I can offer!' ***Go to 96.***

72

'Here we are, guv!' Bert suddenly shouts down after he
has transported you some half-mile from Old Nell's
Music Hall. 'Here's the Dirty Duck tavern just up
ahead! See its name on that large lantern 'anging over its
door?' You and Mr Meek can just see 'Dirty Duck' on
the lantern – but what you can't see is Flaxby's cab.
Does that mean he's already gone? Just as you're

running towards the tavern to peer in through one of its misted-up windows, however, Flaxby suddenly emerges from it. He at once recognises you and quickly lifts his cane. At that moment, though, a policeman appears out of the fog ahead, whistling to himself as he saunters along. Snarling at you, Flaxby races off in the other direction. *Go to 15.*

73

Flaxby's dart just misses you both as you quickly pull Mr Meek down below the seats with you a second time. ''Ere, you two!' a man shouts from behind, angrily grasping your necks. 'Stop causing such a commotion or I'll knock both yer blocks off!' In actual fact, this man probably saves your lives. For, looking down at all the attention you have suddenly attracted, Flaxby obviously decides that firing a second dart would be too much of a risk. You see him immediately leave the box. As soon as you and Mr Meek have managed to wrestle yourselves free of the irate man's hands, you hurriedly find the exit and make your way out of the music hall yourselves. *Go next to 33.*

74

You walk warily down the centre of the massive cathedral, worried that Flaxby might be waiting for you behind one of the tombs or statues. At every moment you're expecting the tip of his cane suddenly to be revealed! Fortunately, you *don't* spot his cane . . . but you don't spot Flaxby himself either. Maybe he's keeping well hidden until he sees you leave again. So you and Mr Meek do eventually leave – but then you

stealthily return by a much smaller side entrance. 'You see those three men sitting in the pew over there?' Mr Meek whispers as you peer out from behind the nearest tomb. 'One of them might well be the contact Flaxby has come to meet here. Which do you think we should keep under observation?'

If you have circled the S in your score card's 📓 *column, you may consult the SKETCHBOOK accessory now to find out which of these three men you should watch. If not, you'll have to take a risk:*

If man reading bible   go to 31
If man in prayer   go to 147
If man admiring roof   go to 125

'I hope you're right about it being the man sitting at the table,' Mr Meek whispers with concern as you both keep your eyes on him from across the room. 'Look, the other two men have wandered off and disappeared amongst those aisles of tall bookcases over there.' The longer you watch this man, though, the more you doubt whether he is Flaxby's contact. Certainly Flaxby hasn't suddenly stolen up to his table yet! 'Well, he must be in the library somewhere *by now*,' Mr Meek remarks in a panic. 'Quick, let's cross over to those aisles and locate the other two men again. For all we know one of them could be talking to Flaxby this very moment!' *Go to 47.*

You dearly hope that your choice was the correct one. For the other two men soon walk away from this spot. The minutes tick by, though, and still Flaxby hasn't appeared to approach this man sitting on the wall. Suddenly, though, his sinister-looking silhouette does slowly come towards him. You and Mr Meek desperately look for somewhere from which you can safely observe the two men. 'Quick, in here, Mr Meek!' you call, noticing a little door in the bridge's huge tower. It's the entrance to the bridge's operating room – and, luckily for you, someone forgot to lock it! *Go to 26.*

77

You at last seem to be approaching Grimble's, the apothecary's. How do you know? Because you suddenly make out Flaxby walking ahead of you through the fog! Or, at least, you *think* it's Flaxby. 'It certainly looks like his purposeful stride,' Mr Meek remarks as he squints through his glasses. Your employer concentrates on the cloaked figure so hard, however, that he strays too close to the kerb and suddenly stumbles noisily into the road. Now you definitely know that it's Flaxby. For he suspiciously swings round and immediately aims his deadly cane at you . . .

Delete the top number in your score card's ☠ column to record this attempt on your life. If you survive it, go to 86.

Some quarter of an hour has passed since Bert waved you goodbye but still you haven't spotted Flaxby on this side of Trafalgar Square. Indeed, you haven't seen anyone at all through the thick clouds of fog. You were hoping that you might at least have noticed Flaxby's contact by now, even if not Flaxby himself! 'It looks as if we should have waited for him on the *north* side of the square,' Mr Meek says, anxiously looking at his pocket watch. At that very moment, though, you just make out

someone appearing from the north side of the square. You both desperately peer after this hazy figure as it slowly disappears again into the fog. Is it Flaxby?

If you have circled the N in your score card's  *column, you may consult the NOTEPAD accessory now to help you work out whether this is Flaxby. If not, you'll take a risk:*

> *If follow figure   go to 124*
> *If disregard him   go to 42*

79

Fortunately, the chestnut-seller must have moved slightly as Flaxby fired his cane over his shoulder because the dart just missed you and Mr Meek. You hear Flaxby curse at him before quickly loading a second dart. At least, you'd *assumed* Flaxby would be loading a second dart but, when you anxiously glance back again at the brazier, you see that he has vanished. He clearly has far more important things to do! *Go to 58.*

80

Travelling in this easterly direction, you and Mr Meek anxiously peer at every shop-front you pass. Through the billows of fog, you're just able to make out a newsagent's, a jeweller's, a locksmith's . . . but still no pawnbroker's. It's when you glimpse a signpost reading *Tower Bridge – ¼ mile* that you both agree that you should go no further in this direction. Flaxby surely wouldn't have headed right the way back to Tower

Bridge. It would have meant that he had gone in one big circle! 'No, he would certainly have planned his route much better than that,' Mr Meek remarks as he leans out of the front of the cab to call up to the driver. 'I think we'd better make our way back to St Paul's and try northwards this time.' *Go to 40.*

81

Fortunately, Flaxby aims his dart just a fraction too low and it strikes the balcony in front of you. It would have been disaster otherwise because you certainly didn't have time to leap out of the way! You do have a little time now, though, and you both dash back to the stairway before Flaxby can reload his cane. You quickly descend the stone steps, taking several at a time, knowing that it is essential you reach the bottom before Flaxby finds his way to them. 'We seem to have made it!' you exclaim, panting, as you finally reach the cathedral's ground level again. 'Let's hurry through this exit door and wait for Flaxby outside in the fog. We'll have much better cover out there!' *Go next to 36.*

82

'We've made it!' Mr Meek says, gasping for breath, after you have spent the last fifteen minutes running all the way from Trafalgar Square. You're now right beneath the jagged, hazy outline of the Houses of

Parliament. 'The message on that beer-mat said that Flaxby's rendezvous here wasn't until half-past eight,' he pants, 'that's another good few minutes! But, of course, our big worry is at which end is that rendezvous likely to take place. Will it be at this Big Ben end or at the other end, near Victoria Tower?'

Which end will you choose?
   If Big Ben end   **go to 53**
   If Victoria Tower end   **go to 30**

83

'Was that Lord Flaxby or not?' Mr Meek whispers after the dark figure has passed your doorway. 'I kept my back to him, pretending to be looking at all the pipes in the tobacconist's window!' Unfortunately, you had been doing exactly the same, worried that you might be seen, otherwise. 'What are we going to do?' you ask in a panic. 'Should we start to follow the man who's just passed – or should we follow the one that he was talking to?' Your employer seems just as unsure as you do . . . but then he suddenly notices a small puddle on the

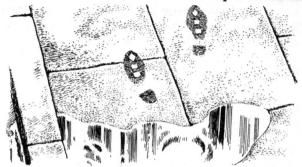

pavement, with a damp footprint just after it. The print had obviously been made by the shoe of the man who just passed!

If you have circled the N in your score card's *column, you may consult the NOTEPAD accessory now to see if Flaxby's shoe would leave prints like this. If not, you'll have to guess which man to follow:*

    If follow man that just passed   **go to 9**
    If follow other man   **go to 106**

84

'We just made it to the cover of this tomb in time!' you gasp as you and Mr Meek flop, trembling, behind it. 'A fraction of a second later and I'm sure Flaxby's dart would have struck one of us!' But the danger is hardly over yet. Flaxby and his lethal cane are still out there! 'When I count to three we'll make a dash the rest of the way to the exit,' Mr Meek says, panting nervously. 'We'll be much safer if we wait for Flaxby *outside* the cathedral and start tracking him again from there.' **Go to 36.**

85

It's not long before this man is the only one left sitting at the bottom of the column. For the other two soon walk away from it. To your dismay, though, the man with the begging-cap comes straight towards you both, asking for a spare copper! Mr Meek quickly gives him a whole pocketful of coins so he'll immediately continue past. You don't want his loud voice giving you away when Flaxby arrives! And very soon, you and Mr Meek quickly pull each other back into the fog as you hear slow footsteps approaching the man still sitting at the base of the column. The hazy newcomer is just recognisable as Lord Flaxby! **Go to 7.**

86

'I'm sorry about giving us away like that,' Mr Meek cries as he hurries towards where you flattened yourself on the pavement. 'The dart didn't graze you, did it?' You assure him that it didn't, though, quickly brushing yourself down. 'Flaxby seems to have hurried off, fortunately,' you remark, as you check the grey swirls of fog ahead of you. 'Just to make sure, though, let's wait here a minute or so. We should be able to find Grimble's without him now.' And so it proves – for the little apothecary's shop is only about another quarter of a mile away. From a dark doorway on the opposite side of the street, you peer through the shop's dim window, just able to see Flaxby conversing with its owner . . .
Go to 12.

87

Fortunately, the little dart just misses you, embedding itself in the back of your seat. And, just as fortunately, Flaxby doesn't linger in the box to try a second shot. Your loud gasp had drawn too much attention! 'He's leaving the box,' you quickly exclaim to Mr Meek, pointing to the disturbance in the curtains behind it. A dark silhouette is hurriedly slipping out between them. 'In fact, he's almost certainly now leaving the music hall altogether,' you add. 'We'd better leave ourselves – this very instant!' *Go to 33.*

88

'We'd better leave this crypt as quickly as possible,' you urge Mr Meek, tugging him after you. 'Flaxby's probably already hurrying to one of the other grids above us, so we're a closer target!' Your fear is justified because you soon spot the soles of his shoes through another grid in the ceiling. But by this time you're both back at the stairway that leads out of the crypt. A couple of minutes later, you're out of the cathedral altogether. You decide that it would be much safer to wait for Flaxby a short distance away from it, hidden by the fog! *Go to 36.*

Thankfully, the fog at last starts to lift a little. This means you're able to drop further back as you continue to follow Flaxby. 'Do you see how he's stopped glancing over his shoulder every so often?' Mr Meek whispers. 'That means he must think he has successfully shaken off any pursuers.' Turning the very next corner, though, you both almost walk straight into Flaxby! He has stopped to question a passer-by. Fortunately, he has his back turned to you and so you have time to take cover. You can either slip into a nearby doorway – or hide behind a beer-barrel cart just away from the pavement.

Which will you choose?
 If doorway   go to 45
 If cart   go to 6

You decided to hail the cab approaching from the right because the horse looked a lot more energetic. 'Liverpool Street railway station, my good fellow,' Mr Meek instructs the driver as you both quickly squeeze through the folding door into the half-open carriage. As the vehicle rumbles off into the fog, you notice a street map of London lying on the black leather seat. It must have been left by the previous passenger. 'Well, it's lucky for us that he did forget his map,' Mr Meek remarks, 'because in our great hurry I forgot to bring my own!'

You are now entitled to use the MAP accessory. Circle the M in the ☙ column of your score card so you have a reminder of this whenever the MAP is required. Go next to 66.

91

The tobacconist's doorway is some twenty metres to the right of the coffee house. 'Ah, a very clever choice!' Mr Meek remarks as you both slip within its shadows. 'We're just near enough to be able to hear if anyone leaves the coffee house . . . but just far enough away not to be spotted by them!' It's not long, in fact, before you do hear footsteps coming out of the coffee house. No, it's not one pair of feet but two . . . *Go to 153.*

Squinting through the fog, you and Mr Meek study every shop-front your cab passes. To begin with, they're all a disappointment – but then you just make out three brass balls hanging above one of the shops in the haze ahead. That's the traditional sign for a pawnbroker's! When you're able to make out the name 'Partridge' above the door as well, Mr Meek immediately orders your cabbie to stop. 'I can't see any customers in there at the moment, can you?' he asks as you both tensely peer through the shop's dim window. 'So it looks as if we've somehow beaten Flaxby to his destination. We'll wait secretly in this cab for the scoundrel to arrive!' *Go to 136.*

It's very possible that Flaxby *did* see you when he glanced up because he now moves about down there more awkwardly than ever. 'You see how he keeps edging towards those pews?' Mr Meek whispers. 'I'm sure something has been *left* for him there – but he's now nervous about picking it up.' If Flaxby is nervous about you, though, you're both even more nervous about him! 'I'm worried that he might suddenly come up that stairway after us,' you tell Mr Meek apprehensively. 'Or at least he'll fire one of his darts up here. I think it would be wise if we quickly made our way back down to the ground level and then slip outside the cathedral to start tracking Flaxby again from there.' *Go next to 36.*

94

You and Mr Meek decide to search the top floor of the library now, actually *passing* the cloaked figure as you climb the stairs. 'I'm positive that wasn't Flaxby,' you remark in a low voice as you stealthily glance back at it. 'He surely wouldn't risk drawing so much attention to himself . . . by keeping on his hat, I mean!' But then you suddenly hear the mysterious figure *stop* on the stairs below you. Then you hear it turn and make a swift movement. 'Look out, Mr Meek!' you suddenly cry out with alarm after swinging round. 'It *is* Flaxby and he's about to fire one of his darts at us!'

Delete the top number in your score card's ☠ column to record this attempt on your life. If you survive it, go to 49.

95

Flaxby angrily pushes the beggar away when he holds out his cap to him. But the beggar is very insistent, grabbing at Flaxby's sleeve. This time Flaxby seizes the poor man by the neck and almost throws him to the ground! Waiting until they have both gone, you and Mr Meek hurry up to the spot where this tussle occurred. You'd noticed an envelope drop from Flaxby's pocket when he grappled with the beggar! Although the envelope's contents have been removed, it's still very incriminating. For, above Flaxby's name and address, is a Ruvanian stamp!

Well done. Record this piece of vital evidence collected in your score card's ✐ column. Go to 123.

You had feared that finding Flaxby's cab again would be like looking for a needle in a haystack. But, a couple of streets further on, your cabbie is calling down to you once more. 'Looks like your friend is a music hall gentleman,' he says as he points proudly towards Flaxby's stationary cab. It's on the other side of the road, directly in front of the illuminated façade of Old Nell's Music Hall. After paying your cabbie his fare and a good tip, you and Mr Meek both hurry up to the music hall's entrance doors. 'Flaxby's obviously meeting his *next* contact in here,' your employer remarks eagerly as you join the short ticket queue. 'The difficult part,' he adds with a concerned frown, 'is are they likely to be meeting in the stalls or the circle?'

Which will you choose?
If stalls   go to 116
If circle   go to 150

You and Mr Meek both keep your eyes fixed to the small hole in the row of books, tensely watching all those who descend the stairway. 'What a shame we can't quite see their faces,' you comment softly after some time. 'Still, Flaxby definitely can't be *this* one coming down because the man is wearing brown, not black, clothes. Nor this one . . . because it's clearly a woman!' But how about the person who comes slowly down the stairway a minute or so later? He wears black

like Flaxby, has a cloak like Flaxby and carries a cane like Flaxby! Just in case it *is* him you keep your heads well down as the man walks from the stairs to the library's exit. The question is, do you follow him through that exit?

If you have circled the N in your score card's 🗨 *column, you may consult the NOTEPAD accessory*

now to help work out whether this is Flaxby. If not,
you'll have to take a risk:

   If follow man   go to 127
   If ignore man   go to 65

98

The customer now wanders off with his bag of
chestnuts but you and Mr Meek keep your eyes on the
man who sold them to him. You're quite convinced
now that he's not a genuine chestnut-seller! And a few
minutes later you have confirmation of this. His next
customer, suddenly appearing from the other end of
the street, is Lord Flaxby! You quickly step back a few
paces into the fog so that they don't see you during their
conversation. It takes place a lot more quickly than you
were expecting, though. When you cautiously creep
forward a little again, you see that Flaxby has already
gone! *Go to 58.*

99

Realising that Flaxby could spot you from his box at any
moment, you quickly make Mr Meek leave his seat.
'We couldn't be easier targets for him!' you whisper as

you both hurriedly squeeze along your row. Once you
are safely at the very back of the circle, standing at the
exit door, you take another look at Flaxby's box. It's
much further away now but you can just see that a
second silhouette is sitting amongst its shadows –
presumably the man you had been watching. 'As soon
as they've finished their conversation, I'm sure Flaxby
will be on his way again,' Mr Meek whispers to you. 'So
we'll wait here until we see those shadowy figures vacate
the box.' *Go to 33.*

100

Bert has by now driven a good half-mile in a northerly
direction – but he still hasn't found the Dirty Duck
tavern. 'Much further northwards and we'll be right
out of central London,' he shouts down. 'What say you
both to me turning round and trying south of the music
'all instead?' You and Mr Meek anxiously nod your
heads at him. You're convinced that, like all Flaxby's
other assassinations, this next one is planned for
somewhere in the very heart of London! *Go to 55.*

101

You decided to concentrate on this man scattering the pigeon food because it seems a very suspicious thing to do at this time of the night. And in the fog! Surely the pigeons wouldn't be able to see him or his food? The man now stands up and starts to wander away from Nelson's Column. You and Mr Meek are warily following his hazy silhouette when you suddenly have this strange feeling of being watched. Nervously glancing over your shoulder, you can just make out a cloaked figure standing under a lamp at the edge of the square. You can also just make out the cane he's aiming at you!

Delete the top number in your score card's ☠
column to record this attempt on your life. Go to 48.

Although he wasn't quick enough to fire one of his darts at you, Flaxby must have noticed you and Mr Meek as you desperately squeezed along your row of seats. For you hear a sudden movement from the box above you as if he has decided it would be advisable for him to leave the music hall. He's in such a hurry to leave, in fact, that he allows the small bottle he was toying with suddenly to slip from his hands. It lands on an empty seat near you and Mr Meek and you both eagerly push your way towards it . . *Go to 41.*

Tower Bridge at last closes again and your hansom cab starts to rumble across it towards the south side of the Thames. 'Is there any point in continuing this journey, Mr Meek?' you ask despondently. 'Surely we'll never catch up with Flaxby now?' Mr Meek still has a little hope, though. 'Did you hear, when Flaxby's cab was just about to speed off the cabbie shouted down to him and checked on his destination? We didn't have time to get particularly close, of course, but I'm sure I heard the cabbie shout something like "Lamp Street Library". That's where I'll ask our cabbie to go!' Unfortunately, though, your cabbie doesn't know of any Lamp Street Library . . .

If you have circled the M in your score card's  column, you may consult the MAP accessory now to find out the rough direction of Lamp Street Library from Tower Bridge. If not, you'll have to take a risk:

If order cabbie south	*go to 67*
If order cabbie east	*go to 8*
If order cabbie west	*go to 132*

104

Flaxby's dart just skims your hair and strikes the tavern window. The loud crack against the glass immediately brings the furious landlord and most of his customers out into the street. "Ere, what the bloomin' heck's going on?' he shouts. 'Who's responsible for this?' You quickly point to Flaxby's silhouette in the distant doorway, seeing this as the best means of deterring him from firing a second dart! And it works! He immediately runs off into the fog. *Go to 15.*

105
Joining the back of the hansom cab queue, you and Mr Meek anxiously count the number of people between you and Lord Flaxby. 'Ten!' Mr Meek whispers to you with alarm. 'This is disastrous. By the time it's our turn for a cab, Flaxby will be a good half-mile away and we'll have lost him. I know what!' he suddenly exclaims, eagerly snapping his fingers. 'You creep up right next to him and secretly listen for the destination he tells his cabbie. You'd better be quick, though – because he's stepping forward for a cab right now!' *Go to 152.*

106

Fortunately, the other man's footsteps are still just about audible and you both quickly make your way past the coffee house towards them. 'Ah, there he is!' Mr Meek exclaims as you now spot the man through the fog. 'And it's definitely Flaxby,' he adds with a shiver. 'Look, he's discreetly flipping open the top of his cane to have a peer down it. The scoundrel must be checking that the dart inside is inserted properly!' *Go to 89.*

107

The man wanders towards the other end of the bridge, frequently checking his pocket watch. 'I've just thought of another possible reason for the flowers,' Mr Meek whispers in your ear excitedly as you both keep some distance behind him. 'They might be a secret signal to help Flaxby identify him!' A few moments later, though, you're both proved completely wrong about the flowers. They *were* for the man's sweetheart. For a young lady suddenly appears on the bridge, running up to him to give him an embrace! You both quickly turn round to search for those other two men who were waiting on the bridge . . . *Go to 151.*

108

Flaxby suddenly turns away from the pew when he sees that he has been spotted. He immediately disappears in the direction of the stairway which leads up to the dome. You and Mr Meek let him go, more interested for the moment in that Bible that has been left for him. As you eagerly snatch it up from the pew, a small envelope falls out from between its pages. *For Lord Flaxby* is scribbled across the envelope's front – and inside it there's a wad of Ruvanian banknotes! Having put this important piece of evidence in his pocket, Mr Meek suggests that you now immediately leave the cathedral. 'We'll wait for Flaxby just outside where we'll be much safer,' he says as he anxiously peers upwards. 'He's probably climbing up into that dome so he can secretly fire his darts down on us!'

Well done. Record this piece of vital evidence collected in your score card's 🔍 column. Go to 36.

109
Tracking this man through the fog, you both edge as close as you dare to try to get absolute confirmation that he is Lord Flaxby. 'Yes, it must be him!' Mr Meek suddenly exclaims in an excited whisper. 'Look at this

train ticket which has just fallen from his pocket. It's a return ticket to Cambridge! Yes, that's our man all right. We'd better slow up a little so he doesn't guess that he's being followed.' ***Go to 89.***

110

You find the stairway that leads up to the dome and both climb the spiral stone steps very warily in case Flaxby is just round the next corner. You at last come out into the narrow walkway that runs round the inside of the dome. 'This, I believe, is the famous Whispering Gallery,' Mr Meek remarks after he has recovered his breath. 'No sign of Flaxby here, though. He must be somewhere below after all. Never mind – this gallery gives us a wonderful bird's-eye view of most of the cathedral!' ***Go to 18.***

111

What a shame you hadn't been more suspicious about the feet! For a few seconds after you have lowered your eyes from the ventilation grid, the person standing there quietly crouches down over it. Then he pokes the end of his cane through one of the holes. It *is* Flaxby after all! Fortunately, his cane makes a slight sound as he pushes it through the grid and you look up just in time. Or are you in time . . . because Flaxby already has his thumb on the cane's silver top, about to release one of its deadly darts!

Delete the top number in your score card's 💀 column to record this attempt on your life. If you survive it, go to 54.

112

'Remember, our client described Flaxby as being quite tall and with the bottom part of his left ear missing,' Mr Meek says, panting after you've both hurried over to the head of platform five. You anxiously watch the last of the passengers file past the ticket-collector. Not one comes even close to that description! 'Blow, he must have already left the train!' Mr Meek exclaims in a panic. 'Where should we try now? We'd better make it the hansom cab queue!' Fortunately, your choice was the right one this time. For a man fitting Lord Flaxby's description exactly *is* standing in the cab queue. You both shiver with fear and excitement as you notice his ear! ***Go to 105.***

113

Your fears were well founded because, dashing up to Westminster Bridge, you and Mr Meek just make out Lord Flaxby through the fog. He's leaning right over the bridge, aiming his cane at a small steamboat that's just about to pass underneath it. You can just see the prime minister on the illuminated deck of the boat, preparing to disembark! 'Quick, arrest that man!' you shout to a policeman strolling on the other side of the bridge. 'He's about to kill the prime minister!' The policeman immediately hurls himself at Flaxby, causing him to drop his deadly cane into the water. But if the policeman's prompt action saves the prime minister's life, it also costs you your main evidence against Flaxby. Unless you're able to produce some other convincing proof, no one is likely to believe you and Mr Meek!

Well done – you have prevented Flaxby carrying out the assassination. To be absolutely sure of bringing him to justice, though, you'll need SIX strong pieces of evidence against him. If the final tally in your score card's ⌁ column is any less than six, try playing the game again to see if you can improve on it!

114

You decide to allow Flaxby to get some way from the library before rushing out of it yourselves. This is so you don't give away the fact that you're trailing him again. But you hadn't reckoned on the fog thickening even more. Flaxby has vanished already! 'That's it!' Mr Meek wails, throwing up his arms in despair. 'My very first case and I've completely bungled it. Come on – we might as well start the long walk back to Baker Street.' **Go to 51.**

'I'd guessed that you might well need me 'elp again,' Bert explains. 'So I hid me cab round the corner and pretended to be innocently looking at them posters on the front of the music 'all. When that roguish-looking fellow of yours came out again, I got right close to him to listen for where 'e intended to go next. He ordered 'is cabbie to the Dirty Duck tavern!' As you and Mr Meek delightedly follow Bert towards his hidden vehicle, however, you learn that there's just one little problem. Bert has no idea where the Dirty Duck tavern is!

If you have circled the M in your score card's 🐦 *column, you may consult the MAP accessory now to find out the direction of the Dirty Duck tavern from Old Nell's Music Hall. If not, you'll have to take a risk:*

    If direct Bert north   go to 100
    If direct Bert west   go to 38
    If direct Bert south   go to 72

Having bought your tickets for the stalls, you slowly make your way down past one row of seats after another. You warily scan each of the rows, looking out

for Flaxby's erect back. 'I think that might be him!'
Mr Meek suddenly whispers to you. 'Do you see? Four
rows further down. The one talking to that rather
hunched-looking man with thick curly hair. We'll take
these two empty seats in this row here so we're not too
close to them!' *Go to 24.*

117

'Yes, he's our man all right!' Mr Meek remarks as you
continue to peer down on this cloaked figure. 'Look
how suspiciously he's standing there. Ah, he's starting
to move at last. Let's hurry round to the other side of the
gallery so we keep him in view.' You're both so intent
on following this man's movements, however, that you
completely disregard the various other people beneath
you. When you do finally give them a quick glance, you
notice that one of them is Lord Flaxby! And he's obviously sensed your presence up here because he has his
cane aimed directly at you, and is just about to fire . . .

Delete the top number in your score card's 💀
*column to record this attempt on your life. If you
survive it, go to 81.*

Tower Bridge proves very easy to find. You soon spot
its white towers looming up through the thinning fog.
When you've reached the bridge, Mr Meek leads you
slowly on to it. 'My guess is that Flaxby has arranged to
meet someone here,' he says, peering from side to side
through his little spectacles. 'So we could do with trying
to work out who that person is and then keeping a close
eye on them. Ah, there are three likely possibilities over

there. They all appear to be waiting for someone. But I
wonder which is waiting for Flaxby!'

If you have circled the S in your score card's 🐟
*column, you may consult the SKETCHBOOK ac-
cessory now to find out which of these three loiterers
is waiting for Flaxby. If not, you'll have to guess:*

If man on left   go to 2
If man in centre   go to 76
If man on right   go to 52

You catch your breath as this suspect suddenly spots the person he was looking for in the audience. Your eyes tensely follow him as he walks down past each row, then finally turns in at one. It's nine rows in front of you – the very row in which Mr Meek had suspected Flaxby might be sitting! But he ignores the empty seat next to the man you've been watching, squeezing right past him until he reaches a woman in a feathered hat. It was merely his girlfriend he was aiming for! There's a smile on your face as your eyes lift up from this couple . . . but it immediately turns to a look of horror. From the shadows of one of the private boxes on the far side of the theatre, you notice a cane suddenly protrude. The evil weapon is pointing straight at you!

Delete the top number in your score card's 💀 *column to record this attempt on your life. If you survive it, go to 87.*

120

You've travelled about a third of a mile in a westerly direction when your cabbie suddenly brings his horse to a halt. He leans down to speak to you both. 'Now I come to think of it,' he says, 'I *do* know which direction ol' Partridge's is in. I once 'ad to pawn my watch there after a bad night at cards. I 'ad these four jacks, you see, and I was absolutely positive they couldn't be beaten. So I bet me whole week's earnings. Well, ye'll never believe it, one of the other players has four –' But Mr Meek politely interrupts him, asking if he could turn his cab in the right direction for Partridge's as quickly as possible! ***Go to 40.***

121

You keep your eyes fixed firmly on this pair of hands. If they make a sudden movement towards the cane propped up near them, you want to be ready! A few seconds later, they *do* make a sudden movement – and you quickly force Mr Meek to duck right below the seats with you. But then you realise that the stage curtain is starting to rise and that the hands were merely preparing to clap! Unfortunately, your dramatic movement attracts the attention of the occupant of a box on the opposite side of the theatre. And you don't turn your head to notice this until that shadowy occupant has his cane ready to fire at you!

Delete the top number in your score card's  *column to record this attempt on your life. If you survive it, go to 73.*

122

You haven't walked far in this northerly direction when Mr Meek suddenly points out a cloaked figure a short distance ahead of you. 'Do you think we've caught up with Flaxby?' you whisper tensely as you peer at this hazy silhouette through the fog. You frantically grab each other's arms as the figure abruptly stops and reveals the top of a cane from underneath his cloak. No, it's not a cane. It's a truncheon. The cloaked figure is just a bobby on his beat! You both immediately run up to the policeman, asking if you're heading in the right direction for Grimble's, the apothecary's. 'No, you should be heading west rather than north,' the policeman replies. 'You want to take the long road at the next left turn.' ***Go next to 77.***

123

Although Flaxby is lost in the fog once more, you and Mr Meek don't worry too much because this time of course you know his next destination. It's the Houses of Parliament. Indeed, it suddenly occurs to you both that the Houses of Parliament are probably not just his next destination but also his *final* one! You should have realised much sooner. *The Houses of Parliament* . . . where better to head for if you intend to assassinate a government minister! So you and Mr Meek both dash round to the Whitehall side of Trafalgar Square and start to hurry along this wide road towards the Houses of Parliament. *Go to 82.*

124

You follow the sound of this person's footsteps as he
walks further and further away from the empty square.
They echo eerily through the night. The echo then
seems to sound rather different. Or is it that another set
of footsteps can suddenly be heard in the fog? You
nervously glance over your shoulder, wondering if
someone has started to follow *you*. The fog seems quiet
and innocent, though. No, it doesn't. You can now just
make out a hazy figure in its midst – and the figure is
quickly lifting an arm from under his cloak. It's Flaxby
aiming his evil weapon at you!

Delete the top number in your score card's ☠
*column to record this attempt on your life. If you
survive it, go to 32.*

125

'Yes, he's the one most likely to be Flaxby's contact!'
Mr Meek whispers with excitement as you both fix your
eyes on this man. 'He's now pretending to be admiring
the cathedral's stained-glass windows but I reckon he's

really looking out for Flaxby!' You hope Mr Meek's assumption is correct because first the man in prayer, then the one reading the Bible, rise from the pew and wander elsewhere in the cathedral. Your employer's assumption *wasn't* correct, though. For a couple of minutes later, something suddenly makes you swing round. Thirty metres behind you, the man who had been reading the Bible now has Flaxby at his side! And they both wear an evil sneer as Flaxby quickly aims his cane at you . . .

Delete the top number in your score card's ☠ *column to record this attempt on your life. If you survive it, go to 46.*

126

'A very good choice,' Mr Meek exclaims when you have led him to the doorway of the barber's shop – on the other side of the road to the coffee house. 'You might make as clever a private detective as me one day!' Was your choice such a good one, though? You are certainly well hidden from the coffee house but is your view of it clear enough? As the fog quickly grows even denser, the figures emerging from there become little more than hazy silhouettes. 'I'm sure one of *those two* must be Lord

Flaxby!' Mr Meek suddenly whispers in a panic. 'But which one? We're going to have to try to work it out quickly because the two men are walking off in different directions!'

If you have circled the N in your score card's 🐝 *column, you may consult the NOTEPAD accessory now to help you identify which one is Flaxby. If not, you'll have to take a risk in deciding which man to start following:*

If man on left   go to 109
If man on right   go to 61

Waiting a half-minute or so after the man has stepped out of the library, you and Mr Meek then rush up to the exit yourselves. 'Oh no, we waited just a bit *too* long!' Mr Meek cries as you both run one way and then another along the street. 'The fog seems to have completely swallowed that man up!' It's then that you hear one of the library windows being quickly opened above you. The two of you look up just in time to see a cane being poked through the opening . . . a cane that is obviously about to fire a dart at you!

Delete the top number in your score card's ☠ ***column to record this attempt on your life. If you survive it, go to 155.***

'Yes, the one with folded arms does look the most sinister of the three, doesn't he?' Mr Meek whispers, agreeing with your choice. 'Look, he's wandered away from that aisle and is now strolling towards the *Famous Crimes* section. Let's follow him!' So you creep towards the *Famous Crimes* section yourselves and both quickly select a book there so you can hide your faces. You're just peeping over the tops of your books at the

man when you hear a spine-chilling cackle some ten
metres behind you. It's Lord Flaxby and he has his cane
raised at you, about to fire one of his darts . . .

Delete the top number in your score card's ☠
*column to record this attempt on your life. If you
survive it, go to 10.*

129
Bert sets you down on the north side of Trafalgar
Square, wishing you luck before driving off into the
night. You and Mr Meek both edge nervously forward
through the thick fog towards the centre of the square,
wondering if Flaxby might have arrived there early.
'Well, he doesn't seem to be here yet himself,' Mr Meek

whispers as he peers through the dense, eerie haze. 'But
what do you reckon about those three shadowy figures

sitting at the foot of Nelson's Column? There's surely a good chance that one of them will be the person Flaxby is due to meet!'

If you have circled the S in your score card's  *column, you may consult the SKETCHBOOK accessory now to find out which of these three figures you should keep under observation. If not, you'll have to take a risk:*

If man on left	*go to 101*
If man in centre	*go to 16*
If man on right	*go to 85*

130

You haven't followed the man far when you have to jump quickly into another doorway. He suddenly stops, fumbles with his cloak and takes something from his jacket pocket. You soon hear his footsteps start up again, though, and you discreetly start following him once more. It's as you're passing the spot where the man had paused that Mr Meek notices a tiny silver box lying on the pavement. It appears to be a gentleman's snuffbox! ***Go next to 154.***

131

'All right, north is it, north it is!' the cabbie shouts down as he cracks his whip over your carriage. Ten minutes later, though, he makes his horse stop and shouts down to you again. 'Just had a word with one of the cabbies going the other way,' he yells. 'Apparently, Garrick's Coffee House is *south* of the station. I'd better quickly turn us round!' You and Mr Meek look despairingly at each other, convinced that you'll now have lost Lord Flaxby completely. But after your carriage has rumbled half a mile or so in this opposite direction, Mr Meek suddenly lets out a gasp of excitement. ***Go next to 25.***

132

Although your journey is delayed even further because one of the cab wheels works itself loose, you at last find Lamp Street Library. 'I was hoping it wouldn't be too big a place,' Mr Meek sighs as you both step down from the cab. 'But look at it – the building's got three huge floors. Finding Flaxby in there isn't going to be as easy as I thought!' Entering the stuffy and dimly-lit building, you agree that you should pretend to browse amongst the books. You can then move furtively from aisle to aisle. But *on which floor* do you do this browsing?

If ground floor   **go to 11**
If first floor   **go to 143**
If second floor   **go to 37**

133

You both hurry over to the station's newspaper stand.
'Excuse me, my man,' Mr Meek says to the vendor.
'But have you recently served someone who's missing
the bottom part of his left ear?' This, your client had
said, was the most distinctive feature about Lord
Flaxby. Unfortunately, though, the vendor says he
hasn't served such a person – or not that he's noticed.
'Our last hope is the queue for the cabs, then,' Mr Meek
says in a panic. As you're both approaching the cab
queue, Mr Meek suddenly pulls you back. 'There's
Lord Flaxby!' he exclaims nervously and excitedly.
'The man second from the front of the queue. Look at
his ear!' *Go next to 105.*

134

You and Mr Meek quickly step behind a statue of a
politician as the figure starts walking towards you again.
When it has passed you and the sound of footsteps
has completely faded, you rush out to pick up a ball of
paper that you saw the figure toss into a nearby litter-
bin. 'So that *was* Flaxby!' you exclaim as you unfold the
piece of paper. 'Listen to this: *After deed executed,*

return immediately to Liverpool Street station. Lie low at my Cambridgeshire estate until other agents get in touch. These must have been the notes Flaxby made when he met his last contact! So, Mr Meek, it wasn't so important that we were at the wrong end for the meeting after all. And this scrap of paper is a valuable piece of evidence against him as well. All the police have to do is prove that it's Flaxby's handwriting!'

Well done. Record this vital piece of evidence collected in your score card's 🔍 column. Go next to 58.

135

You both make your way to the stairway that leads down to the cathedral's crypt. The massive stone tombs in there include Nelson's, the Duke of Wellington's and Sir Christopher Wren's and, normally, you would doubtless have stopped to admire them. This time, though, you're much too worried about your safety. Flaxby and his lethal darts could be waiting for you behind any one of those tombs! As it turns out, you discover that you're the only ones in the crypt. Flaxby must be above you somewhere. 'You don't think that's him directly above us, do you?' Mr Meek whispers with

sudden anxiety when a pair of feet appear over one of the ventilation grids in the crypt's ceiling. 'Perhaps he could pick up our voices beneath him and he heard his name mentioned!'

If you have circled the N in your score card's  column, you may consult the NOTEPAD accessory now to help you work out whether this is Flaxby. If not, you'll have to take a risk:

If assume it is Flaxby   *go to 63*
If disregard person   *go to 111*

136

You don't have to wait very long for Flaxby's arrival. Tensely peeping out from your stationary cab, you soon watch his driver pull up outside the pawnbroker's shop and then Flaxby's sinister silhouette sweep through the door. Only a minute or so later he's emerging again, jumping back into his hansom cab. But instead of immediately speeding off as you'd been expecting, the cab silently waits there for a while. 'It's a good job we got here first,' Mr Meek says to you with a sudden shiver. 'I've just realised what he's up to. He's waiting there to see if we're still following him. I dare say he has his cane all ready to fire from inside that vehicle!' *Go to 44.*

137

You manage to find the apothecary's shop fairly easily. But you and Mr Meek don't rejoice, because you can see no sign of Flaxby through the dim window! 'Let's just hope it's because he took a rather longer route than us,' Mr Meek says anxiously as you hide in a dark doorway directly opposite the small shop. Your anxiety is soon relieved, however. A few minutes later, Flaxby's dark silhouette appears at the shop door and, after a quick, furtive look round, he steps inside . . . *Go to 12.*

138

Your cab at last reaches Liverpool Street station – but are you too late? You and Mr Meek rush up to one of the porters at the station and ask if the Cambridge train has arrived yet. 'About five minutes ago,' the porter replies. 'There she is – over on platform five.' Hurriedly turning your heads, you see that most of the train's passengers have already left the platform! There remain just a few stragglers, still making their way towards the ticket-collector. Should you rush over to platform five in the hope that Lord Flaxby is amongst these stragglers? Or would you do better to search for him elsewhere in the station – perhaps at the newspaper stand or in the hansom cab queue?

Which will you choose?
If platform five	*go to 112*
If newspaper stand	*go to 133*
If hansom cab queue	*go to 13*

139

You let out a huge sigh of relief. The footsteps belong to a man with blond hair, not black. He might be dressed very like Flaxby . . . but it isn't him! You wonder why you haven't heard a sigh of relief from Mr Meek as well. Turning to him, you see that it is because he has his eyes tightly closed! 'It was a false alarm, Mr Meek,' you say, chuckling softly. 'This man isn't Flax —' But then you pull your employer sharply back so the man hides you both from view. Flaxby *has* now appeared on this floor, and is striding quickly from the bottom of the stairway to the library's exit. *Go to 114.*

140

'Well, that man's definitely waiting for someone even if it's not for Flaxby,' Mr Meek whispers after you have quietly made your way down the second aisle. 'Listen to how he's anxiously pacing around in the next aisle. Can you hear him through the shelves? Hush!' he adds, suddenly putting a finger to his lips. 'Someone's now coming along the aisle to join him!' You and Mr Meek press right against the shelf of books, desperately straining your ears to try to hear what this newcomer says to the man. Although his speech is very muffled, you can both just identify the word *Ruvania*. There can be absolutely no doubt about it now. This newcomer is Flaxby! *Go to 39.*

141

Taking a notepad from his pocket, Mr Meek starts to write down his various observations about Lord Flaxby. He seems quite proud as he does this. He's sure it's exactly the sort of thing that Sherlock Holmes would do! 'These details will be invaluable to us,' he says as he hurriedly jots down one observation after another. 'You see, people are generally very consistent in their various habits. For instance, if a person takes his left glove off first on one occasion – just as we noted Flaxby do a few moments ago – then he'll usually do so on *every* occasion.' Mr Meek suddenly has to finish his jottings, though, because Lord Flaxby is now right at the front of the cab queue. You quickly walk up to it yourselves!

You are now entitled to use the NOTEPAD accessory. Circle the N in the  *column of your score card so you have a reminder of this whenever the NOTEPAD is required. Go next to 105.*

142

You both hurry down one empty street after another, desperately trying to spot Flaxby. 'Is that him?' you suddenly ask after you've just turned a corner. 'Yes, it could be,' Mr Meek says, panting, as you both peer at a dark figure in top-hat and cloak who is tying up his shoe-lace. 'I hope that business with the shoe isn't just an act of his,' he adds anxiously. 'Perhaps he *heard* us running after him and wanted to trap us!' Your employer's concern proves justified because the figure suddenly points his cane in your direction and fires a dart from it. You both leap back round the corner – but only just in time!

Delete the top number in your score card's ☠ *column to record this narrow miss. Go next to 89.*

143

Climbing the narrow wooden staircase to the library's first floor, you and Mr Meek start to scan the aisles for Flaxby. You look from one row of tall bookcases to another. 'He's certainly not anywhere on *this* floor,' Mr Meek whispers with concern. 'He's either on the floor above or below us – or he's already gone!' It's then that you notice a cloaked figure making his way down from the floor above. Unfortunately, though, he still has his hat on and keeps his head well down as he slowly

descends the stairs. Without moving any closer to the stairway, it's hard to tell whether this is Flaxby or not . . .

If you have circled the N in your score card's  *column you may consult the NOTEPAD accessory now to help you work out whether this is Flaxby. If not, you'll have to take a risk:*

If follow cloaked figure	*go to 23*
If disregard him	*go to 94*

144

'There's still no sign of Flaxby stepping out to join him,' Mr Meek comments softly after you have both crept as close to the collection box as you dare. 'Perhaps his

Mr Meek's reference to the Bible suddenly makes you think. The man's not holding it any more! You urgently swing round and peer back at the other end of the cathedral, where the man had been sitting. You spot Flaxby edging towards that pew, just about to go and pick up the Bible that has been left for him there! *Go to 108.*

145

'Quick, back in the cab!' you shout at Mr Meek as the dart just misses your arm, bouncing off the cab's side. 'Flaxby must be hidden in one of those vehicles over there!' It's soon obvious *which* vehicle. For, as you and Mr Meek hurriedly climb into your cab and sit right back in its shadows, one of the hansom cabs on the other side of the road suddenly speeds off into the fog. Although it has a good start on you, your own driver quickly gets up a reasonable speed himself, managing to keep Flaxby's vehicle just in sight. *Go to 71.*

146

As excited as Mr Meek, you quickly take the beer-mat from him and study the tiny instructions. They read: *Meet Trafalgar Square contact at 8.00 and Houses of Parliament contact at 8.30. These contacts will give you final details for your assignment.* Barely a minute later, Bert's cab is speeding you towards Trafalgar Square, rattling through the foggy night. This is one destination he does know! But, although you reach Trafalgar Square well before eight o'clock, you're dismayed at how thick the fog is here. You can see only about halfway across the square. So it's absolutely essential that you guess the right side for Flaxby's secret rendezvous!

Which side will you choose?
 If north side   go to 129
 If south side   go to 78

147

The man in prayer suddenly opens his eyes as you secretly observe him and then walks slowly towards the other side of the cathedral. 'We'd better follow him,' Mr Meek whispers as the man now makes his way towards the main exit doors. 'I'm sure he's Flaxby's contact!' But just as you're about to walk out into the fog again, you suddenly get a strange feeling that makes you want to turn round. *There's Flaxby's cane*, poking out from behind the broad plinth of a statue! And it's obviously just about to despatch a dart!

Delete the top number in your score card's 💀 *column to record this attempt on your life. If you survive it, go to 84.*

148

You very carefully tail Flaxby as he walks swiftly away from Grimble's, the apothecary's, hurrying down one street then another. He seems to be heading back towards the Thames, travelling in a northerly direction. In fact, he goes even further than that: his cloak swirling across Blackfriars Bridge and disappearing round corner after corner until he reaches the massive looming silhouette of St Paul's Cathedral! *Go to 43.*

149

'Did this man have a top-hat and cane?' Mr Meek asks the flower-girl eagerly. 'And was he dark and quite tall?' You both grin with relief and delight when the woman nods her head. 'Well, that was a very dangerous man you were talking to,' Mr Meek tells her. 'And because he's so dangerous, it's essential we keep on his tail. So quickly, please tell us the way to Grimble's, the apothecary's as well!' This time, though, the woman shakes her head. 'But that's just what I was telling this rude gent,' she says. 'I've never heard of no Grimble's apothecary's shop. You should have 'eard his curses as he ran off to find someone else to ask!' So you and Mr Meek are immediately sent into despair again. Which direction do you try for the shop?

If you have circled the M in your score card's
column, you may consult the MAP accessory now to
find out the direction of Grimble's shop from Lamp
Street Library. If not, you'll have to take a risk:

If head north	*go to 122*
If head south	*go to 20*
If head west	*go to 137*

150

Buying tickets for the circle, you and Mr Meek hurriedly make your way up the stairs. 'Take your seats immediately, please,' the man at the circle entrance tells you. 'The entertainment is about to commence.' As soon as you've sat down, you quickly scan all the other members of the circle audience before the lights are dimmed. 'Is that Flaxby nine rows in front of us?' Mr Meek whispers uncertainly. 'It's so hard to tell from the back. I suppose he could equally well be that one *eleven* rows in front!' But if Flaxby is hard to identify, maybe his contact here isn't. For you notice that three

late arrivals have appeared at the back of the circle. They're each obviously looking for someone before taking a seat. Is one looking for Flaxby?

If you have circled the S in your score card's
column, you may consult the SKETCHBOOK
accessory now to find out which of these three late
arrivals is Flaxby's contact. If not, you'll have to
guess:

If man on left	*go to 119*
If man in centre	*go to 70*
If man on right	*go to 35*

151

'Well, the man sitting on the wall is still there,' Mr Meek says with some relief as he peers across the bridge. 'We'll just have to hope he's the one we want!' You keep this man under observation for a good ten minutes, though, and still he sits there alone. But then a dark figure slowly approaches him. 'Look, it's Flaxby!' you exclaim. In your excitement, you can't help pointing . . . and, unfortunately, Flaxby notices this. The next thing you know, one of his deadly darts is flying just over your head!

Delete the top number in your score card's ☠ column to record this near miss. Go next to 26.

152

Quickly sidling up to Lord Flaxby, you carefully listen as he steps into his cab. You're sure he mutters the destination 'Garrick's Coffee House' to the driver. 'I wonder which direction that is,' Mr Meek says thoughtfully when you have returned to him. 'Oh, well, I'm sure our cabbie will know.' When your turn for a hansom cab comes at last, however, you find that the driver has no more idea of how to get to Garrick's Coffee House than you two do! 'There's no Garrick's Coffee House to the east of the station 'cos that's where I live,' he tells you. 'So that leaves north, west or south. Unless you've got a map with you, you'll 'ave to take pot-luck between those three!'

If you have circled the M in your score card's  *column, you may consult the MAP accessory now to find out the rough direction of Garrick's Coffee House from Liverpool Street station. If not, you'll have to guess which direction to order the cabbie:*

    If North   *go to 131*
    If West   *go to 69*
    If South   *go to 28*

153

The two sets of footsteps pause for a while outside the entrance of the coffee shop and you hear a muffled conversation begin. 'There are two men talking, both in top-hats,' you whisper as you carefully peep out from your hiding-place. 'So one of them could well be Lord Flaxby! Quick, press right into the doorway,' you add urgently. 'The two men have now separated and one of them is coming straight this way!' *Go to 83.*

'This snuffbox must have fallen out when the man put his hand into his pocket,' Mr Meek remarks as he examines it closely. Opening the lid, he finds a tiny inscription engraved on the inside. His short-sighted eyes suddenly light up with excitement. 'Now we have proof not just that it's definitely Lord Flaxby ahead,' he exclaims, 'but that he *is* in league with Britain's enemy! This inscription reads: *To Lord Flaxby. The Prime Minister of Ruvania gratefully thanks you for all your services!*'

Well done. Record this piece of vital evidence collected in your score card's ✐ column. Go to 89.

Fortunately, the dart just misses you . . . and, fortunately, Flaxby doesn't stay at the library window to fire a second dart. You're sitting ducks down there! 'He must have *heard* us shouting to each other in the street,' Mr Meek gasps after you have both hurried to the safety of a nearby doorway. 'We must be more careful next time,' he adds, his limbs still trembling. 'That mistake of following the wrong man could have cost us our lives!' *Go to 59.*

156

'Right, I think it's safe to come out now,' Mr Meek whispers. 'Let's hope that book contains some information that will be useful to us!' he adds as he hurries over to pick it up. It looks as if it does! The pages contain sketches of several rather unpleasant-looking faces. Underneath each face is scribbled a certain location. 'It's my guess that these are various accomplices that Flaxby needs to make contact with along his route,' Mr Meek remarks excitedly. 'Unfortunately, though, he's almost certainly got another list of them on his person somewhere because this looks like only a draft copy!'

You are now entitled to use the SKETCHBOOK accessory. Circle the S in your score card's
column so you have a reminder of this whenever the SKETCHBOOK is required. Go next to 22.

Collect all six titles in this series: